The Words We Use

COLLECTION 3

The Words We Use

COLLECTION 3

Diarmaid Ó Muirithe

FOUR COURTS PRESS

Set in 10 on 12 Bembo
and published by
FOUR COURTS PRESS LTD
Fumbally Lane, Dublin 8, Ireland
e-mail: info@four-courts-press.ie
and in North America by
FOUR COURTS PRESS
c/o ISBS, 5804 NE Hassalo Street, Portland, OR 97213.

ACKNOWLEDGEMENT

These articles are reproduced from the *Irish Times*,
by kind permission of the Editor.

© Diarmaid Ó Muirithe 1999

A catalogue record for this title
is available from the British Library.

ISBN 1-85182-466-9

Printed in Ireland
by ColourBooks Ltd, Dublin.

For Mary,
the dark lady of Sanderstead Avenue:
coelesti luce crescat.

Abbreviations

EDD	*English Dialect Dictionary*
OED	*Oxford English Dictionary*
UDD	*Ulster Dialect Dictionary*

Contents

Hogmanay

Hogmanay is, all the evidence tells us, more popular now than it has been for centuries; the Scottish countryside on New Year's Eve is as lively as it was when Rab Burns was kicking his heels with his Jean or with Mary Morrison or whomever was handy.

Hogmanay, the word, has intrigued lexicographers for a long time. The first gentleman to chance his arm in print about the word's origin was the formidable Calder, a staunch believer in the wrath of God, who wrote in 1694: 'It is ordinary among the plebeians to go about from door to door upon New Year's Eve, crying Hagmana! a corrupted word from the Greek *Hagla-mana*, which signifies the holy month.'

The word is of French origin. In the dialect of Normandy they had *hoquinano* and *haguinelo*, cries on New Year's Eve. In Caen, *hoguillanao* was a New Year's gift.

It should be remembered that hogmanay also had this meaning in Scotland; children went around the houses begging, and one of their rhymes was: 'Hogmanay, trololay, Give us of your white bread and none of your grey, Get up an gie's our hogmanay.'

Not all was fun and games on hogmanay. In western Scotland, *Napier's Folk-lore* (1779) tells us: 'All household work was stopped, the yarn reeled and hanked, and wheel and reel put into an outhouse. The house itself was whitewashed and cleaned. A block of wood was put on the fire about 10 p.m. so that it would be burning briskly before the household retired to bed. The last thing done by those who possessed a cow or horse was to visit the byre or stable, and I have been told it was the practice with some, twenty years before my recollection, to say the Lord's Prayer during this visit.'

Nothing much has changed. In parts of the North this is still done before the family goes back to the fire to wait for the first-footer and the guisers.

A happy new year to you – and a good hogmanay.

Grogue – Spock – Rickle

'There they were, groguin' on the sofa with the lights out.' That was sent to me by a gentleman from Thurles who writes to me frequently and who signs his letters Mary Willie (Mary Willie's is a famous Tipperary pub, in case you don't know). *Groguin'* is what's troubling him.

Had my friend asked around the bogs of Tipperary they would have told him that a *grogue* is a 'foot' of turf, three or four sods standing on end like a little pyramid on the turf bank to dry. It's from the Irish *gróig*, which as a verb also means huddle. That is what my friend's couple were doing on the sofa.

A more comfortable position than the one mentioned in Ó Dónaill's dictionary by way of elucidation: 'Bhí siad gróigthe ar bharr an bhalla' – they were perched together on top of the wall.

The great Dinneen, every vigilant in case somebody might think that 'they' were people and up to no good, would have added: 'as do birds'. (He always used the present tense instead of the infinitive, which gave his dictionary the following beauties: 'I give birth to a still-born calf', 'I copulate, as of swine'.)

An interesting word from the bogs of Donegal is *rickle*. Michael Barrett from Dunlewey gave me this one recently. The *Ballymena Observer* (1892) tells us that rickles are 'peats put to dry with a foundation on their ends, and others built on their sides on top of the foundation. A rickle differs from a clamp in being long and narrow instead of circular.'

Ó Dónaill gives the Irish as *ricil*, but the word's origin lies elsewhere. It's in Scots as *rickle* and in northern English as *ruckle*, and it surely has a Norse origin. There is a Norwegian dialect word *rygla*, which means a small lose heap, and another one, *rukle*, a little heap of firewood. These are also related to another Ulster word, *raughle*, a heap of stones; a badly built stone wall.

Burns had young Mr Barrett's word. In his *Epistle to J. Laprail* he wrote: 'May Boreas never thresh your rigs, Nor kick your rickles aff their legs.'

My thanks to Patrick Fennessy of Gurrane, Ballyhea, Charleville, for his comments on *spock*, Irish *spaic*, an inferior hurley. Inferior the *spocks* might be, but that didn't stop Mr Fennessy's grandmother's uncle from being transported to Australia for cutting the makings of one on the Castleoliver Estate, near Kilfinnane. Words are indeed fossil history.

An Ark of a Woman – Doory – Ganch – Flegg Off

An old hill farmer from west Cork once described Dolly Parton to me as a little ark of a woman. I know I'm wronging the man, and the Irish language, by spelling the word as *ark* instead of *earc*; the practice of composing quasi-phonetic anglicised spellings for Irish words is a contentious one and I won't go into the rights or wrongs of it here.

I doubt if Ms Parton would be very pleased to be compared to a newt; neither am I sure that she would forgive the Gweedore man who called her a *doory* wee lass in my presence not long ago. *Doory* means very small. I am reliably informed that Ms P is indeed diminutive when viewed from the rear, but the word's origin might annoy her.

Doory is the same word as Middle English *dwery*. In a poem from about 1440 we find: 'Now as a crepil lowe coorbed doun. Now a duery and now a championn'. *Dwery* is an inflected form from Old English *dweorh*, a dwarf.

Róisín Kelleher is a charming woman who works for the BBC in Belfast. She sent me the word *ganch*, which she says is a silly person.

Ganch, also found as *gansh*, *gaunch*, *gunsh*, is also a verb meaning to stutter; to talk in a halting, agitated way, according to the excellent *Ulster Dialect Dictionary*. It also means to talk stupidly; to bite, snap. As a noun, *ganch* also means a stammer; a snap; a loudmouth; an inarticulate person.

But as to the origin of the word, all we know for certain is that it's a Scots import, and probably onomatopoeic.

The UDD doesn't have the verb *fleg* as R.N. Watson of Dunmore, Co. Antrim has it. 'My mother used to say, "Oh, fleg off wi' ye" when she wanted us out from under her feet. I am quite certain that it was not a vulgarism, but please can you show any light on the word's origin?'

The Scottish dialect dictionaries have this *fleg*. One glosses it as 'to flutter, to flit from place to place'. I can quote you R.L. Stevenson's *Catriona*, which has: 'The Solan understood about knives ... He gied ae squawk and flegged off.' But as to the word's origin, ne'er a one of the dictionaries I have hazards a guess.

If I may be so bold, I think it's from Old English *flegan*, the same as Old High German (*ar-*) *flaugan*, to put to flight.

Marmalade – Spire – Birl

J. Gallagher of Deramore Park South, Belfast, wrote to ask about the word *marmalade*. He has heard that it has connections with Mary Queen of Scots.

There may be some folkloric connections with the poor woman, but marmalade is from the Middle French *marmelade*, from Portuguese *marmelada*, from *marmelo*, quince, from Latin *melimelum*, from Greek *melimelon*, a word composed of *meli*, honey, and *melon*, apple.

Micheál Ó Máille from Cullina, Beaufort, Co. Kerry, reminds me of the word *spadhar*, pronounced spire, more or less, used by Liam Ó Muirthile in a beautiful piece he wrote recently about the Munster Blackwater. This Irish word for the reeds used by thatchers is an importation. The English is *spire*, a name given to various course kinds of rush or sedge, the thatchers' *Phragmites communis*.

One glossary of New Forest words speaks of spire-beds, 'places where the spires or shoots of the reed-canary grass grow that are used by plasterers and thatchers in their work'. Spire is an old word. It's in *The Owl and the Nightingale*, written about 1225; it speaks of 'spire and grene segge'.

Mr Ó Máille also sent the word *birl*, heard in Glenflesk, near Killarney, Co. Kerry. It means a trip or a short quick journey there. I'm surprised to find this word so far south. It's onomatopoeic, and Scots in origin, and is found all over Ulster in the senses to spin, to go fast. 'Give it a birl', means give it a try, in places I know near Glenties, Co. Donegal.

There is another *birl* still in use in Donegal, and for all I know in other places in Ulster. To be *on the birl* means to be 'on the batter'. This may be connected with the spinning notion associated with over-indulgence; I don't think so, however.

Birl, also written *birle* and *burl*, is found all over Scotland and the north of England in the sense to pour out liquid, to pass it around, to ply somebody with drink. It also means to go 'on the tear'.

A lady in Scott's *Minstrelsy* 'birled' a man with her ale and wine. In *St Ronan*, the same writer has 'he gaed down to birl it away at their bonnie bottle'. I've heard *birler* near Dunfanaghy, Co. Donegal, for a drunkard.

Now this *birl* is not related at all to the spinning, travelling *birl*. It's from Old English *byrlian*, to pour out, to give to drink; related to Old Norse *byrla*.

Skeel — Teach

An old Wexford friend of mine, Paddy Murphy, the Enniscorthy potter, died recently. Years ago David Shaw-Smith made a beautiful film about him and I helped out as best I could with the script. The last time I met him Paddy gave me some words connected with his craft and advised me to collect words that belong to other crafts near extinction.

Professor Gordon Quin of Trinity College, Dublin, members of whose family were coopers in Guinness's brewery, gave me a few words of his father's. One of them was *skeel*. You'll find it in many of the glossaries of English and Scots dialects; the *Concise Ulster Dictionary* has a few *skeels* but not this one.

It is described in various glossaries as a wooden pail, wooden bucket, a tub, a shallow wooden vessel. In Durham it was described as a peculiarly shaped bucket, formerly used in colliery villages to carry water for household use. They were carried on women's heads, and a piece of wood was made to float to the top to prevent overspills.

In the farms around Shakespeare's birthplace, the *butter skeel* was used for working the butter in by pressing it with the hand, as the *dough skeel* was used for kneading bread by hand. In Gloucestershire *skeels* were used for setting milk in, to stand for cream; Marshall's *Rural Economy* (1789) informs us the *skeels* were made in the tub manner, with staves and hoops, and two stave handles, and that they were various sizes, from 18 in. to 2 ft 6 in. in diameter, and from 5 to 7 in. deep. In both Gloucestershire and Northumberland the *skeel* was also used to cook beer.

What it was used for in Guinness's long ago, I'm afraid I've forgotten. At any rate *skeel* has been associated with Viking ale for a long time. The Old Norse was *skjóla*, a wooden bucket.

And how about this for a survivor? Down in the Lobster Pot in Carne, my favourite Wexford watering hole, an old man once asked me to *teach* him his pint. He wanted me to reach across and to hand it to him. Teach is from Old English *taecan*, in the meaning 'to show something to somebody'.

That was 30 years ago. I doubt if the old word has survived modernity's baneful influences.

Callow – Kalish – Tetters

Dr Leslie Lucas of Rosapenna, Co. Donegal, wrote quoting from an article he read lately: 'The unmistakable rasp of a corncrake from across the callows'. What is a *callow*? he asks.

A callow is a low-lying damp meadow by the banks of a river. An Irish river, I might add, for callow is confined to Ireland, though to what parts of Ireland I'm not sure. P.W. Joyce doesn't give the word: neither does *The Concise Ulster Dictionary*. But the following turns up in Coulter's *The West of Ireland* (1862). 'The extensive callows lying along the banks of the Suck'; and in a report in the *Dundee Advertiser* in August 1883 its Irish correspondent informed readers that 'all the callows on the banks of the Shannon to Lusmagh are submerged'.

The EDD has the word and so has the OED, but neither offer an etymology. The word is from Irish *caladh*, a riverside meadow (Dinneen). The anglicised form escaped the nets I cast when compiling my *Dictionary of Anglo-Irish*;[1] I am grateful to Dr Lucas for it.

I am grateful, too, to Mr Tom Murray of Wexford town for another word that should have been included in my dictionary. He overheard a west Cork woman giving out to her daughter for wearing jeans that artfully displayed her bare knees and tantalising bits of her bottom: 'You are noting but a *kalish*,' said the ageing matron. It's the Irish *ceailis*, a slattern.

1. Four Courts Press, Dublin 1996.

A travelling woman came to my door the other day, selling holy pictures. She was young, and had a little girl with her. When I attempted to give her daughter a few bob to buy ice-cream, the mother stayed my hand: 'the child had the tetters', she said: *tetters* (mostly used in the plural by travellers) means ringworm.

The EDD makes no mention of Ireland in its entry relating to it, but the ancient word, from Old English *teter*, ringworm, is common in rural England. In many places *tetter* means any kind of small pimple or pustule. *Tetters* on the tongue were thought to be a punishment for lying. And as for the *tetter* dreaded by adolescents, these pustules euphemistically called 'spots' in the television advertisements, well, if all fails, why not try this old Cornish charm: 'Tetter, tetter, you have nine brothers. God bless the flesh and preserve the bone. Perish, tetter and be gone, in the name of the Father, the Son and the Holy Ghost.'

Author or Authoress? — Gooseberry Fool — Silly

Mrs Mary Clancy from Portmarnock asks: 'Should I, or should I not, use *author* and *poet* when I want to refer to females who write?'

I have noticed that the suffix - *ess* in *poetess*, *authoress* and *actress* is used less and less in print these days, both in the newspapers and in the literary reviews. Anthony Burgess noted that those responsible for this business still found *princess*, *duchess*, and *countess* perfectly acceptable; even *mistress* they had no desire to tamper with. Nor, he said, were they averse to clicking their fingers to get the attention of a humble *waitress*. I am informed that in one American university it is now considered offensive to women to refer to a Greek *goddess*.

It's a matter of choice for the moment, Mrs Clancy. But *poetess* and *authoress* seem to have had their day. Custom is the sole arbiter of verbal propriety, as Horace said; and a very capricious power it can be. The - *ess* is from French -*esse*, used to denote a female person or animal, from Late Latin *issa*, from the Greek -*issa*.

I'm glad to see those words ending in -*ette* falling into disuse. *Usherette* is one. It wasn't coined until around 1925. *Usher* is related to *os*, the Latin for mouth, and *ostium*, the mouth of a house, otherwise the door. From *ostium* came *ostarius*, a doorkeeper. In Old French, it was shortened to *hussier* which gave English *usher*.

A lady from Thurles wants to know the origin of *fool* in gooseberry fool. Is it related to the other fool, a silly person, she asks? It seems to be, and suggested by the synonym *trifle*, mentioned by John Florio in his Italian-English dictionary of 1598: 'Mantaglia – a kinde of clouted creame called a foole or a trifle in English.' Fool is as interesting as it is old. *Flo* is the Latin for 'I blow', and it comes from *follis*, a bellows. *Follis* found its way into many languages in the sense, originally, of a man who talks a lot of air. The noun *folly* is a little closer to the original Latin. *Silly* is ancient, too, and has changed a great deal over the centuries. First came the Gothic *sels*, good, and after that Old English *saele*, happiness. The adjective *seely*, ancestor of *silly*, came to mean favoured by heaven, afterwards holy, then harmless, then simple, then simple-minded. All, of course, related to the modern German *selig*, blessed.

Spock – Putalogue – Smut – Hangnail

It would embarrass me to tell you how long ago Dermot Treacy of Strandhill Road, Sligo, wrote to me about a word remembered from his boyhood in Kilmallock, Co. Limerick – *spock*, a word a friend of mine also heard as *smock* in Bruree. Mr Treacy writes: 'During the war it was hard, and expensive, to get a hurley. We used to play on the main Kilmallock to Kilfinnane road with improvised hurleys which we called spocks. I haven't been able to find the word in any Irish dictionary.'

Can anybody help with this word? I have no idea where it originated.

I can do better with *putalogue* for Anne Walsh of Ballygunner in Waterford. She tells me that it means a plump woman or a plump boy where she was raised, out Mullinavat direction. She has never heard a fat man called a *putalogue*; there's a cuddly something about the word, she feels.

Putalóg is the Irish, and it's onomatopoeic. The late R.B. Walsh of University College, Dublin, and Slieverue, Co. Kilkenny, gave me the word. He heard it in west Waterford. Diarmaid Ó hAirt's *Diolaim Déiseach* glosses it as a fat chicken. They have *putachaun* in south Galway. There it means both a fat, lazy person and a cuddly young woman.

Grace Hart hails from Fanad in Donegal and she wants to know where an expression 'Take that smut of your face' comes from. Her mother would use it when one of her offspring got into a bit of a sulk about something. *Smut* is Irish; a sulky expression, a pout, according to Dinneen. Michael Traynor's *The English Dialect of Donegal* has the phrase *Domhnach na Smut*, 'the Sunday of the frowning faces, the first Sunday of Lent, from the discontented appearance of the women who did not get a man'.

The word *hangnail* is also bothering Grace. They call it *agnail* in parts of Scotland, she says.

Yes, there are many names in the dialects for this minor irritant; *backfriend, stepmother's blessing, fan nail, nang nail* and *thang nail* among them. The Old English was *ang-naegl*; the original meaning seems to have been a corn on the toe, a painful, compressed nuisance that must have felt like an iron nail. *Ang* meant compressed, tight. Compare *ang* in *angmod*, anxious, *angness*, anxiety. *Naegl* was an iron nail. *Hangnail* came from the popular, mistaken, association of *naegl* with the nail that grows on the fingers.

Kippeen – A Proper Tike – Slops

From Happy Valley, South Australia, Dymphna Lonergan wrote to inquire about some words of Irish provenance she has come across in the writings of Miles Franklin. One of the words she is in doubt about is *kippeen*, and this doesn't mean a twig; as Dymphna says, it was used in the context of a suicide and seems to refer to the rope mark around the victim's neck: 'So it's the nasty kippeen av a divil's collar he dresses wid.'

I think the only part of that word that's Irish is the diminutive, *een*. The *kip* in question was, very likely, imported from England, where it is still found in Yorkshire, Norfolk and Somerset; I've never heard it in Ireland. A country word, it means the skin of a young animal used for tanning. It's an old word.

'Kyppe of lambe a furre' was recorded in an English tract of 1530.

The word's origin is uncertain, but you might compare the Low German *kip* and the Middle Dutch *kip* and *kijp*.

'A proper tike' is a phrase James Reilly, a Monaghan man who wrote from Aldershot, sends me. He remembers tike being used at home when he was young. *Tike* or *tyke* is in general dialect use in Scotland, Ireland and northern England and means a dog, a hound, a cur and, figuratively, a rough, ill-mannered person.

It is also applied to mischievous, tiresome children and, in Leeds, to men who chase women and to women who chase men. That it is the Shetland word for the common otter gives a clue as to its origin, the Old Norse *tik*, a bitch. *Piers Plowman* has the word: 'But vnder tribut and taillage as tykes and cherles.'

Lastly, Anne Reid from Santry asks me if I ever heard the Dublin word *slops* used for the drawers with long loose legs recommended by reverend mothers to their pupils in days of yore. Before my time, Anne; but the word is in the English dialect dictionaries, sure enough.

Shakespeare had it too. In *Much Ado about Nothing*, don Pedro refers to 'a German from the waist downward, all slops'. He had large wide trousers in mind in this case, but he would have called any loose outer clothing slops. You may remember Mercutio saying: 'Signior Romeo, bon jour! There's a French salutation to your French slops.' From Old Norse *sloppr*, a loose trailing garment.

Kibes – To Milder – Healer

'Her shins were dotted over with fire blister, black, red and blue; on each heel a kibe.' So wrote Carleton in his *Traits and Stories*. *Kibe*, as far as I know, is not found in the south of Ireland. It means a chilblain, a crack in the skin, as the man who sent me the word, Mr Jack Smith, of Monaghan, well knows: he is interested in the word's origin.

In the *Ballymena Observer* (1892), we are told that 'those suffering from kibes get rid of them by going at night to someone's door and knocking. When anyone asks "Who's there?" the person who knocked runs away, calling, "Kibey heels, take that." Then the kibes are expected to leave the person who had the disease and pass to the one who called "Who's there?"'

Mr Smith may be interested to know that the word is not confined to the north of Ireland. It is also found in East Anglia, Somerset, Devon and Cornwall, as well as Wales, where it came from in the first place. Master Shakespeare used the word in *Hamlet*: 'The toe of the peasant comes so near the heel of the courtier, he galls his kibe.' The word is from Welsh *cibi*.

Mr Jim Sutton, an old school friend from New Ross, asks about the verb *to milder*, to rain heavily.

This was originally a milling term: the milder was the quantity of corn ground at one time. Figuratively, milder (in some places *melder*) came to mean a great flow, a large quantity, a deluge. It's from the Old Norse *meldr*, flour or corn in a mill.

From Janet Hall, of Naas, comes a query about the word *healer*, a horse's cover or rug. The verb *heal* means to hide, to keep secret. A healer is one who hides or conceals anything, such as loot in foreign banks; in southern England they have a saying 'a healer's as bad as a stealer'. To heal also means to cover up; hence Mrs Hall's healer. Hence too a word I heard many years ago from Mr Bill Blake, a fisherman from Kilmore Quay, *healing*, by which he meant a coverlet.

In the north of Ireland, *to heal* means to cover with a slight layer of earth; to plant cabbages in a temporary way, to keep them safe until it is convenient to plant them permanently.

All these are from the Old English *helian*, *helan*, to cover, hide, conceal.

Tent – Honcho – Figairey

Writing from a Dublin hospital and asking for anonymity, a nurse would like to know the origin of the word *tent* as used in medicine. *Tent* she describes as a roll of gauze that increases in size when wet, used to dilate an opening; it was also used as a probe for searching or cleansing a wound.

My friend wonders if the word is related to the word for the movable shelter made of canvas and supported by poles.

The medical tent came to use in the 14th century from the Old French *tente*, from *tenter*, to try, to examine. It meant a probe, and its ultimate origin was the Latin *temptare*, to try, to test. And so it's related to *tempt*, to allure, to attempt to persuade to do something.

Shakespeare, in *Troilus and Cressida*, has: 'Modest doubt is call'd The beacon of the wise, the tent that searches To the bottom of the worst.'

He also uses *tent* as a verb meaning to probe; in *Coriolanus* he wrote: 'Well might they fester gainst ingratitude And tent themselves with death.' But the word also meant to cure, to heal; again in *Coriolanus* he has: 'For 'tis a sore upon us you cannot tent yourself.'

The canvas tent is from Old French *tente*, from Latin *tentorium*, something stretched out, from *tendere*, to stretch.

J. Taylor from Sutton wonders where the slang word *honcho*, the boss, comes from. He (or is it she?) knows Spanish and, having failed to locate it in Spanish dictionaries, wonders if it is some South American dialect word.

The word is American soldiers' slang and is no older than the Korean War. But it is not Korean in origin, but Japanese. *Han* is what we in Ireland would call a *meitheal*, a number of friends or neighbours who would take on such jobs as saving each other's crops. The word was transferred to military work units. *Cho* is leader. Hence *hancho*, or *honcho*, the leader of a work unit.

And lastly, my guess as to what *figairey*, a whimsical notion or fancy, comes from, I think it's a dialectal variant of *vagary*, ultimately from the Latin *vagari*, to wander. It's not confined to Ireland as the EDD would have us believe; Chris Renton, who lives in Blackberry Lane, Delgany, has it from his native Yorkshire. Monica Ryan from Limerick asked about it a few months ago. Sorry for the delay.

Hurry-burry – Fonogue – Coharrying – Carbuckling – Pickeering

Heather Bell live in Santry, but her youth was spent in Co. Antrim. From there she remembers some interesting usages of the word *hurry*.

First of all there was the compound *hurry-burry*, confusion entailing a lot of noise and commotion. She also remembers the phrases *take your hurry* and *take your hurry in your hand*. Both of these mean take your time.

A *hurry* could also mean a pressure of work. Heather's mother used to say: 'Don't bother me now. Don't you see I have a hurry?' This too was a Scots import. The *English Dialect Dictionary* quotes a Dumbarton source for the following: 'I lend a hand when the smith has a hurry.'

A *hurry* also means a row, a fight, in Antrim, not necessarily a violent affair, however. A good scolding would be classed as a hurry in Antrim; in Scotland blood was invariably drawn. In *Lintoun Green*, written in 1695, you'll find the couplet: ''Tween stick and war they kept their feel, The hurry heats their blood.'

I looked up various dialect dictionaries to see if I could add to the various Northern hurries. In W.H. Patterson's *Glossary of Words Used in the Counties Antrim and Down* (1880) we are told that *hurry* 'is a name given to the Irish Rebellion of 1798'. How interesting.

In Lancashire a *hurry* is a spasm, a fit; a fight; an outburst of temper, and in Norfolk, Suffolk and Essex a hurry is a small load of corn or hay brought into the barn or haggard for fear of a downpour of rain. In the Dedham (Essex) Records of 1654 there is warning given to carters: 'No inhabitant of this towne shall cut any grasse in any of the common meadows vpon the penaltie of forfeiting ten shillings for every loade or hurry of hay so cutt.'

This word *hurry* is probably of Scandinavian origin. Compare the Swedish *hurra*, to whirl.

Down in St Mullins, Co. Carlow, recently, an old friend bought me a drink and instead of saying cheers! or *sláinte!* said *fonogue! – fan óg*, of course, stay young. I note that Séamus Moylan has this too in *The Language of Kilkenny*, attributed to a man from Kilmoganny. Remember that now if you are tempted to try *coharrying* or *cubuckling*, throwing your arms around a woman; or even *pickeering*, making romantic overtures to her. These too are from Dr Moylan's 300-page treasury of Kilkenny words. Their origins are obscure.

Juge – Fantasheemy – Doolally

I don't usually tackle questions about placenames, preferring to leave these matters to Flann Ó Riain to deal with in his column, but I couldn't resist a plea from Ms Anne James of Mountgarry, Swords, Co. Dublin. She has been trying without success to find an explanation of the name of a cul-de-sac leading to the Broadmeadow river at Swords – Juckback Lane.

This was once called *Jugebage* Lane, Anne tells me; it was referred to as such in the Civil Survey of 1651: 'three acre called Jugebage'. In this *juge* lies the answer, I feel.

Juge is merely an old spelling of *jug*, an obsolete word for a common pasture or meadow. Worlidge's *Dictionarium Rusticum* of 1681 has it, as has Bailey's dictionary of 1721. The word is from French dialect *un juge de terre*, and *juge* is from Latin *jugum*, which in this context means as much land as a pair of oxen could plough in a day – an acre approximately.

The *back* in the word may simply mean 'situated behind', but, depending on the terrain, of course, it could have been a survival from Old English *baech*, a valley. Does the land behind the lane slope, I wonder?

Helen Walsh from Sandymount asks about a word her grandmother, who came from south Kilkenny, had. I remember hearing the word used by Mrs Liz Jeffries of Neamstown, Kilmore Quay, long ago; a lady since gone from us.

The word is *fantasheeny*. Liz used to say that some people, lately come up in the world, had such *fantasheeny* ways, God help 'em. What she meant, and what Ms Walsh's granny meant, was that they were showy, and ostentatious in their vulgarity.

How this word came to roost in south-east Ireland is a mystery to me. I have never come across it elsewhere in this country, although it is found in Devon. It's an Italian word, of course; it's the same word as *fantoccini*, little puppets made to move by means of concealed strings. It properly means foot-soldiers. John Florio, Shakespeare's friend, and author of the charming dictionary, *A Worlde of Words*, has '*fantoccio*: a foolish serving creature'.

T. de Róiste from Ballincollig, Co. Cork, would like information about *doolally*; an adjective meaning eccentric, not quite the full shilling. He wonders if it's from Irish.

Ah no. The word was coined from the *Deolali* army sanatorium in Bombay. No prizes for guessing how it came to Cork.

Tory Tops — Wicklow Words

Father Pádraig Mac Cárthaigh of Rathdrum, Co. Wicklow, sent me a few interesting words, some local, some not. The first of these is *tory tops*, heard in Cork; these are pine cones and are known in Galway and in Wicklow as *cogneys*.

The *English Dialect Dictionary* has *tory tops* but doesn't give an etymology. It was one of the few words to be sent to Oxford from Co. Cork. Father Mac Cárthaigh guesses that it is related to Irish *torthaí*, fruits. I don't know. Neither do I know the origin of *cogneys*. I've heard *boorkeens* in Carlow. The Irish is *buaircín*.

When a Wicklow man cleans out or disembowels a rabbit, he *panches* him. This word was known also to Colm Devereux of the Willow Grove and to Michael Donnelly of Corrigower, but not to two young ones of about 20 who sipped a drink in Mr Devereux's pub. Bad news this. I didn't bother asking them what they'd do to a deer; you wouldn't *panch* it, you'd *grollick* it in both Rathdrum and Callary. This is from Irish *greallach*, entrails. Scots Gaelic has the word, too; and Scots English has *gralloch*.

George Mooney from Newtownmountkennedy gave me the word *shoorawns*, and Father Mac Cárthaigh knows of a woman who had, unwisely, cut them with a strimmer and suffered a severe *rash* as a consequence of being hit by flying pieces of the weed known to most of us as hogweed or cow-parsnip.

The Wicklow Irish is *siúrán*. De Bhaldraithe's dictionary gives *odhrán*; McKenna's has *odhrán*, *feabhrán*, *fuarán* and *fleabhrán*; and Dinneen found *fiúrán* in Dublin, a word sent to me in the form *fewrawn* by J. O'Brien of Shankill some time ago.

Cloerauns is another of Michael Donnelly's words. They are heaps of small stones gathered from a cornfield to assist the mower; the cairns are usually built near the ditches in the corner of the field. The word, no doubt, is a local form of Irish *clochrán*.

Lastly, an old use of the word *concern* from Wicklow. I heard it at young Geraldine Magee's wedding the other night. A woman who lives near Geraldine in Corrigower was talking about President Clinton's *concern*. This was her word for an affair. It was a common euphemism in Restoration days. 'It is not long ago that I had a concern with a signora', wrote the dramatist Wilson in *Bolphegor* in 1690. Obsolete everywhere now, Oxford thinks. Tell them that in Wicklow.

Wiseacre — Romany — To Ted

A story related by Brewer in his famously unreliable dictionary tells of Ben Jonson arguing the toss with a snobbish squire. Said Ben: 'What care I for your dirt and clods? Where you have an acre of land I have 10 acres of wit.' The squire retorted: 'Good Mr Wiseacre.'

Brewer was a dab hand at chancing his arm when he hadn't a clue as to the origin of a word or a phrase. Wiseacre is from Middle Dutch *wijsseggher*, a sayer of wise words. Modern German has *Weissager*. Ruth Hall from Craigavon asked about the word.

Some of the people who have taken to philosophising in print and on local radio about the gypsies who have come ashore in Rosslare are a bit confused about the languages they speak, confusing Romanian with Romany. Romanian belongs to the Romance group of the Indo-European family; Romany belongs to the Indic branch of the same family, although it contains many words borrowed from local European tongues. *Romany* means gypsy, and comes ultimately from the Sanskrit *domba*, a musician of low caste. The gypsies will find a lot of *dombas* in some Wexford pubs I know.

George Borrow's engaging book, *The Romany Rye*, means The Gypsy Gentleman. *Rye* is related to Latin *rex*, to the Spanish *rey*, to the French *roi*, to the Hindi *raja*, and to our own *rí*. The Sanskirt root word was *rajan*, king. It's a small world, God knows.

John Burke, a Galwayman living in Manchester, asks about an

expression they used in his youth −*to ted*, which means to turn and spread newly-mown hay to help it dry. I've come across this word in Lover's *Legends* (1848): 'She was all day teddin' the new-cut grass.' The word was once in general dialect use in Scotland, Ireland and England. It's from the Old Norse *tethja*, to spread manure, related to *tad*, dung, and Old High German *zetten*, to spread.

Dr David Sowby of Foxrock reminds me that Shakespeare used the word *tetter*, ringworm, as a noun in *Hamlet*. He used it as a verb in *Coriolanus*: 'So shall my lungs coin words till their decay against those measels, which we disdain should tetter us.' The traveller I heard it from also had it as both noun and verb. Explaining her child's ringworm, she said: 'She got tettered by an oul' ass we have.'

Let On − 'And He Drunk'

A calque is an expression that is a literal translation of a foreign expression −a loan translation. Colm Ó Baoill, professor of Celtic at Aberdeen University, in the course of an essay in the superb *Edinburgh History of the Scots Language*[1] (edited by Charles Jones), teases out the phrase 'to let on', to pretend, but in a negative construction 'divulge' or 'admit' (as in 'Never let on ...' in both Scots and English). In 12th-century Irish, and in the other two modern Gaelic languages, we find expressions of which 'let on', meaning 'pretend', is probably a calque.

The form of the preposition used for 'on' in Middle Irish is the personal one (*form*, 'on me', *fair*, 'on him', etc.). Thus, *léicid fair* would mean 'he lets on him'; now consider that Scots had the modern-sounding 'he is not so daft as *lets on him*' in 1589. But the problem with saying with absolute certainty that 'let on' reached Scots from Gaelic is a gap in the written evidence between the 12th century and 1589. The earliest instance of the negative use (which is not found in early Gaelic) dates from 1629: 'Christ letteth not on him that hee either heareth or seeth me.'

The *Oxford Dictionary* says of both usages that they are 'original

1 Published by Edinburgh University Press at a price I, for one, can't afford −£140 sterling.

dialect and US English': it found that the earliest non-Scottish instances of 'let on' are 1828 for the positive and 1848 for the negative usages, both from America's east coast. If I were Mr Paddy Power [an Irish bookmaker] I would offer you very short odds indeed that the expression 'let on' reached English from Scots through medieval Irish; but modern Irish, operating through American English, may also be a claimant.

And how about the use of 'and' in constructions such as these which I myself have heard: 'You shouldn't be lifting things and you pregnant' (Ireland); 'He drove the car and he drunk' (Galloway); 'You were so good to come to see me and you so tired after your journey' (Lancashire). This use of *agus*, 'and', is found in all three Gaelic languages and in medieval Welsh too. It has been in Irish, Ó Baoill reminds us in his masterly essay, since the 8th century.

The French *calque* means a tracing. You'll hear them by the score if you *give a while* in any part of rural Ireland. Our rich English is liberally garnished with them.

Hurry – Pickeering – Mungledemmery

My thanks to both Séamus Ó Saothraí of Blacklion, Greystones, and Harry Williamson of Ashley Park, Bangor, Co. Down, for pointing out to me that the word *Hurry*, used in allusion to the 1798 rebellion, is found in Florence M. Wilson's celebration of Thomas Russell, hanged in Downpatrick in 1803 – *The Man from God-Knows-Where*: 'In the time of the Hurry we had no lead / We all of us fought with the rest / An' if e'er one shook like a trebling reed / None of us gave neither hint nor heed ...'

Mrs Wilson was born in Lisburn in 1877 but spent most of her life in Bangor. Her only collection of verse was published in Dublin by the Three Candles Press and printed by Colm Ó Lochlainn in a limited edition of 450 copies. I would not be in the least surprised to hear that Ó Saothraí, scholar and bibliophile, has a copy.

He tells me, too, that the word *pickeering*, mentioned here recently, is not confined to Co. Kilkenny. *Pickeering*, if I may refresh your memory, is the act of making romantic overture to a woman. It was, he says, much used in his own boyhood in Co. Westmeath. And in east Ulster (he doesn't say exactly where) the act of putting your arms around a girl and giving her an oul' hoult is referred to as giving her a *Killinchy muffler*.

Breege Cunningham, of Ballinrobe, Co. Mayo, is puzzled by her mother's word, *mungledemmery*, and so, I must confess, am I. This is a mutant parsnip with two roots or legs. I have come across *mungle* in the dialect dictionaries of England, and it may well be related to the first element in Breege's word.

It – and its variant *mundle* – means a stick, often forked, used to stir cream in the dairy. People who visited farmhouses not far from where Shakespeare grew up were always invited in the old days to use the *mungle* in the dairy to deter the fairies from stealing the cream. *Mungle/mundle* are of Norse origin. *Mundull* was Old Norse for a handle.

Mungles are found in various country phrases. *Have a little, give a little, let neighbour lick the mungle*, is one. It means that one should look after oneself first. *I'll have a lick of the mungle before I burn my tongue*, means I will have my pleasure even if I have to suffer for it. And to *lick the mungle* means to curry favour.

But *demmery*, I'm afraid, has me baffled.

Shoddy – Oxter

Mr Seamus O'Brien of Bishopstown, Cork, tells me that he was surprised that his dictionary can shed no light on the origin of the word *shoddy*, except to say that it is of unknown origin.

The adjective is certainly related to the noun *shoddy*, which was a woollen trade term: it mean waste from the carding machine and refuse from worsted spinning mills. The word was, as you'd imagine, found mainly in Yorkshire and Leicestershire, but in Yorkshire *shoddy* was also the noun they used for inferior coal. In Co. Antrim in the last century, shoddy was their word for the smaller stones found in a quarry; these weren't of much value. *Shoddy dust* was what Yorkshire-men and women called the minute wool fibres, mixed with oil and dirt, the refuse of scribbling and grinding machines, used in the manufacture of shoddy. This stuff was sold to Kentish hop-growers, the EDD says. In Antrim, *shoddy flags* were quarried flags of a poor quality; and in Lancashire a *shoddy hole* was simply a rubbish hole or tip. My guess is that the adjective came from the noun; but where the noun came from is anybody's guess.

The word *oxter*, the armpit, intrigues Ms Ruth Blake of Sandycove, who asks if the word is an Irish dialect word.

Oxter is certainly widely used in Ireland, but it is found too all over Scotland. In England it seems to be confined mainly to the north. The EDD has this interesting little quatrain from Antrim: 'Whether would you rather / Or rather would you be, / Legs to the oxter / Or belly to the knee?'

No MacTavish was ever lavish, Ogden Nash assures us; be that as it may, to the Highlander *to come with the crooked oxter* means to come with a present; and in the case of a wife, to bring a good dowry. But oxter also meant the bosom in Scotland; it's as well to know that if you, like me, are fond of Scots ballads; otherwise you'll wonder at wee Jock frae Auchtermuchty, or wherever, taking such an interest in his loved one's alluring oxters. You might also like to know that to oxter a woman means to fold her in your arms and give her a good hoult. Hence the splendid line in an Aberdeen song: 'The foreman's in wi' the Missy, Sittin' oxterin' her in the kitchie.'

A good old word, this *oxter*. The Old English was *oxta*, the armpit.

Spock – Shoddy – Spay

I have to thank Mrs Dympna Moore of Cahir, Co. Tipperary, and Máire Nic Mhaoláin of Dalkey for throwing light on the word *spock*, also found as *smock* in Co. Limerick – an improvised hurley. Mrs Moore quotes from Art Ó Maolfhabhail's *Camán: 2,000 Years of Hurling in Ireland*, published in 1973. He records *spaic aitinn*, meaning furze or whin root, from Cos. Clare, Limerick and Cork. I wonder what the origin of *spaic* is.

Thanks to Louis Marcus for an interesting note about the noun *shoddy*, inferior clothing, now obsolete. It was used by Padraig Pearse in the *Claidheamh Soluis* in 1906. Writing about the 'tendency towards slavish imitation which is the result and the auxiliary of Anglicisation', he went on: 'This hopeless subservient spirit is seen alike in the educated man who despises all things Irish as crude, and the uneducated who picks up the [to him] latest music-hall jingle, in the businessman who thinks the English accent of a commercial traveller is an indication of superior goods and in the farmer who clothes his children in English shoddy ...' Shoddy originally meant the waste from worsted spinning mills, if I may refresh your memory.

Last month a Donegal *spay woman* or fortune-teller of my acquaintance offered to read my palm. I accepted the lady's offer and was told that a dark-haired woman was about to enter my life. *Spay*, more often written *spae*, is found in most of the glossaries on Ulster English. It was imported from Scotland. Burns has it in *Halloween*, written in 1785: 'I daur you try sic sportin, As seek the foul Thief ony place, For him to spae your fortune!'

To *spae by the girdle* (griddle) was a mode of divination practised in Argyllshire for discovering who had stolen something. The girdle was heated red-hot and placed in a dark corner, where something made of iron was laid on it. The entire company had to go, one by one, and fetch whatever was on the girdle, with the assurance that the Devil would burn the hand off the thief. His reluctance to participate betrayed the criminal.

By the way, my spay-woman was right. A week later my grand-daughter, Mary, came into the world in London, sporting a luxuriant head of sable hair. I now await with increasing confidence the fulfilment of the spay-woman's second prediction, that I am shortly to have notable success in the Lotto draw.

Spae / spay is from Old Norse *spá*, to prophesy, foretell.

To Pree – Enteete – Mohawk

The verb *to pree*, meaning to taste drink, and to relish the same, was recorded 120 years ago in Antrim and Down by W.H. Patterson, a contributor to Joseph Wright's great *English Dialect Dictionary*. Richard

Shaw sent me the word from Bangor recently; it was a word often used by his late father, but he hasn't heard it for a long time.

You can *pree* more than the Devil's brew. There is a Scottish version of the proverb which goes, 'To prove the pudding is to *pree* it.'

To *pree* can also mean to kiss, although Patterson didn't record this usage in Ulster. That is what the Scottish poet Cromek (fl.1770) meant when he asked his mot, 'Sweet maiden, will ye pree?' Another poet, the equally bad Jamie, in his masterwork, *Muse* (1810), interesting only for its dialect, wrote, 'He cheered the bonny lass and pree'd her mou'among the grass.'

Pree is a form of *prieve*, to try out, to experience, a Scots and northern English form of *prove*, but from a different part of the Old French verb *prover*, as Caroline Macafee's *Concise Ulster Dictionary* points out. Ultimately from Latin *probare*, from *probus*, worthy.

Another interesting Ulster-Scots word from Ballymena is *ass*. It means fine ashes; in Northumberland it is coal dust, watered to make slack. It's from the Old Norse *aska*.

John Kinsella, from Wexford, asks where the word *enteete* originates. This was a siesta taken by people in the southern baronies of Forth and Bargy. The custom didn't die out until the beginning of the present century. Dr Russell, of Maynooth College, writing in the middle of the last century, suggested the word may 'more properly be *noonteet*' (noontide) — the noontide rest. Professor P.L. Henry, writing in *Lochlann* many years ago, commented it is not easy to see Russell's authority for the emendation, though he thought the explanation plausible enough. He suggests an alternative explanation would take as a starting-point the Old French verb *entoitier*, to shelter (indoors).

'We have a word for big, awkward half-wit: *a mohawk*.' So writes Martin Gladney, of Graigue, Co. Kilkenny. This word was current in the south-east as far back as the mid-18th century, and it got its name, I think, not from the Indian tribe, but from an infamous Dublin street gang of the time. I remember the word used in salutation to certain Kilkenny hurlers, as they took their places against Wexford, in my time.

Spriggan – Muffler

Miss Jane Stade wrote to me from Devonshire recently requesting information about a word used in both Devon and Cornwall, *spriggan*. I can tell her that I have heard her word near Carnsore in Co. Wexford.

Not for the first time I have to draw on a word list I collected from Phil Wall, a man who was 90 or thereabouts when I met him in the late 1970s, having been introduced to him by Mr Leo Carthy, a recent recipient of an honorary degree from the National University.

A spriggan to Phil Wall was an unruly child; the word, according to Wright's *English Dialect Dictionary*, is of Cornish origin, and means a fairy, a goblin. I suppose that Irish people who live outside the barony of Forth in south-east Wexford would find an affinity between the *spriggan* and the *cluthracán*, an unruly sprite known for mischief-making.

This is what *Hunt's Popular Romances of the West of England* (1865) has to say about *spriggans*:

> They appear to be offshoots from the family of the Trolls of Sweden and Denmark. They are found only about the cairns, coits or cromlechs, burrows or detached stones, with which it is unlucky for mortals to meddle.
> They are a remarkably mischievous and thievish tribe. If ever a house is robbed, a child stolen, cattle carried away, or a building demolished, it is the work of the spriggans.
> Whatever commotion took place in earth, air, or water, it is all put down to the work of these spirits. It is usually considered that they are the ghosts of the giants of old; they have the charge of buried treasure.

Another *blúirín* of folklore was recorded in the English *Folk-lore Journal*, vol. 4, 1886: sad to say, the poison of anti-Semitism had even then reached the Cornish tin mines: 'Knockers and Spriggans, and all underground spirits ... always heard working where there is tin, and who are said to be the ghosts of Jews who crucified Jesus'.

Margaret McCann of Newry, Helen O'Neill of Swords, late of Co. Down, and June Baird of Bangor wrote to me giving out about my ignorance in implying that a *Killinchy muffler* was a *male* embrace.

The *Killinchy muffler*, I am now told, was what the *woman* applied to the man. 'The Killinchy men, being cold, slow and useless, are given a hoult round the neck to get them closer; muffler as in scarf, geddit?' explained Ms McCann, who very kindly indeed offered me a demonstration.

Maaley – Mwigley – Clissy – Mothered Water

John McCarthy, who was born near Cappamore, Co. Limerick, wrote to me from London recently about a word often used where he grew up. The word is, as John spelled it, *maaley*, and it was usually heard in the phrase 'acting the maaley', which meant behaving in an overbearing fashion.

Well now, I know about *maaley* due to the generosity of Donal Curtin of Mayrstone Drive, Limerick, who sent me fifteen pages of Irish words used in the English of his county. *Maaley*, he explained, is *meathlaí* in its Anglo-Irish form; and the *meathlaí* was the leader or pace-setter in a *meitheal*, or band of workers engaged in communal activity such as helping a neighbour out at harvest time, or saving his hay or turf. The anglicised form is still to be heard, I'm glad to say.

Another of Mr Curtin's words is *moilgí*, which for the benefit of people whose Irish is rusty or non-existent I'll offer the quasi-phonetic (and not too accurate) *mwigley*. *Moiglí* is an adjective meaning soft, mild. You might refer to *moiglí* weather, or a *moiglí* woman, though not to her face, I should think.

Séamus Ó Saothraí from Greystones sent me the Westmeath *clissy*. This was said to a girl: 'Aren't you the little clissy!' Clissy is *cleasaí*, a trickster. But what, I wonder, is the origin of another of his words, *floovrus*, pudding, custard-and-jelly and the like.

Tom Donnelly, writing from Blackrock, Co. Dublin, tells me that in the Kildare of his youth a sullen, grumpy fellow would be described as *mothered*. Why so? he asks. Molly-coddled by the mammy to such an extent that he didn't mix well with others? No, I've heard people in south Carlow speak of the mothered water of the Barrow when they meant turbid from rain, so the mothers are innocent. Mothered is from the Irish adjective *modartha* (try *motherha*), gloomy.

Up North now, to Bangor, to where Mary Wise has been trying in vain to find the origin of the verb *to feal*. This word, unknown in the south, as far as I'm aware, means to hide, to conceal. It's known all over northern England, as well as in Ulster, but the *English Dialect Dictionary* hasn't recorded it in Scotland. There is a proverb from Cumbria which says, 'Them at feals shall find.' In a tract from 1570 'to feale' is glossed 'abscondere', to hide. *Feal* is from the Old Norse *fela*, to hide.

Addle – Hurry – Curthere

'He *addles* more in a week than you would in a month', an old woman who lived in Meenbanad, in the Rosses of Donegal, said to me once. The word surfaced again last week in a letter sent to me by a retired teacher from Dunfanaghy direction who doesn't want to be named.

Addle is found in England's northern counties and is quite common in various places in the north of this island, which is a little strange at first glance, as the word is not known in Scotland, according to the *English Dialect Dictionary*.

To addle means to earn. There is a riddle from Lincolnshire, quoted in *Notes and Queries* in 1865, which runs, 'Grows in the wood, an' yowls l' the town, An' addles its master many a crown. Answer – a fiddle.' My Dunfanaghy correspondent has also heard the noun *addlings*, though not of late. Addlings were a woman's earnings; money got by selling the odd dozen of eggs or by knitting for the factories or shops.

If the word is not from Scots and is not from Irish or Scots Gaelic either, the chances are it is of Norse origin; and sure enough there's the Old Norse *aethal*, property.

If the men who took part in the War of Independence were said to be 'out', Séamus Ó Saothraí from Greystones reminds me that those who got caught up in the 1798 *Hurry* were said to be *up*. The term was used in Leinster as well as in the North, and Madden, in his *Literary Remains of the United Irishmen*, recalls a song called *Up*. All nature is up, the author claims, and so, 'The progress of this rising rage, No human power can stop; Then tyrants cease vain war to wage, All nature will be UP.'

Curthere was the Forth, Co. Wexford, word for season (Norman French *quarter*, Old French *quatier*). Seamus Heaney told me the other night of an inspector who visited a school in Tyrone's Sperrin mountains during what the Forthmen and the Bargymen used to call *Arragh Curthere* (Irish *Earrach*, Spring). 'Name the four seasons, boy', says your man to a wee scudler who was knee high to a wether. 'Well, sir,' he answered after thinking on it, 'there's the lambin, and the clippin, and the dippin ... and then the tippin.' Full cycle.

Panch – Shoddy – Quilt

Some time ago I mentioned the Co. Wicklow verb *panch*, to remove the entrails from a rabbit. Since then, I have received an interesting letter from Dr Vincent McMahon who practises medicine in Carbonear, Newfoundland. He says *panch* is in everyday use in his part of the world, but that it is 'generally applied to the butchering of moose, several thousand of which are hunted and shot in the woods yearly'.

I forgot to mention the origin of *panch*. It's a variant of *paunch*, itself from Old French *panche* from Latin *pantex*. Jehan Palsgrave in his 1530 *Lesclarcissement de la langue françoyse* has, 'Je paunce, I panch a man, I perysshe his guttes with a wepen.'

Dr McMahon went on to write about the noun *shoddy*, waste from carding machines, refuse from worsted spinning mills, recently mentioned here. No doubt he felt like perysshinge a certain clothier's guttes with a wepen back in the early 1950s, when, 'with my own hard-earned cash I purchased my first suit for a little over £6.

'This was the most dearly-bought clothing I have ever had. The trousers disintegrated in four weeks and the jacket in six. A few years later I could afford to go to a bespoke tailor and I told him of my sad tale. He said, "You bought a suit of shoddy." He told me that shoddy was manufactured in the English midlands from 90 per cent re-teased rugs and 10 per cent wool to bind the short fibres. It was invariably dyed charcoal to hide the light threads and the stuff was purchased only by the very poor for weddings and funerals.'

A bad quilt, no doubt, was the man who sold that suit. *Quilt* is a Dublin word, and it comes from Irish *cuileat*, a knave, or at least I think it does. Mary O'Hara from Boswell Street, London, questions this etymology of mine given in my *Dictionary of Anglo-Irish*. 'What about Shakespeare's quilt in Henry IV, part 1?' she asks: 'How, now, blowne Jack? How now quilt?'

This is merely the word for a thick covering for a bed, humorously applied to a fat person. It's from Old French (12th-century) *cuilte*. I have given thought, too, to yet another quilt but as it has never been attested to outside one English county, I've left it out of the reckoning. It means a boil, a pimple. No, I'll stick to my knave.

Murn – Tooting – Kist – Keech – Hushion – Abide

I was delighted to get a letter from Mrs Catherine Murphy, who has lived all her long life in Ringsend, apart from a spell she spent in Lancashire in the 1950s. 'Liverpool was, in a sense, closer to us than Bray in my young days', she says. 'I wonder would you be interested in some of the words I picked up long ago, some here, some across the water?' Dear Mrs Murphy, what sort of a question is that? I'll let you do the talking.

Murn: This means stuck up. This is a Lancashire word. I've never heard it in Dublin. This is how you'd use it: 'The murn of them people, since they were left a bit of money!' (This is a Manx word, *moyrn*, haughtiness, pride).

Tooting: There are people who, when they come to visit, mooch around the house, picking up things and examining them, opening cupboards etc. You'd say that these people were tooting around. (John Clare has this in the *Shepherd's Calendar*: 'for birds in bushes tooting'. Its origin is Old English *totian*, to peep out).

Kist: A chest. You'd hear a seaman's chest called a kist. (Old Norse *kiste*, a casket, a coffin. Irish *ciste* is a borrowing.)

Keech: A sweet cake. This I heard in Lancashire from the woman

I boarded with. (The *English Dialect Dictionary* has 'Keech: a large oblong or triangular pasty, made at Christmas, of raisins and apples chopped together.' The Irish *císte* is a borrowing from this English dialect word.)

Hushion: This is what many of my Liverpool friends called a cushion. (I once heard an old woman from Horeswood, near Campile, Co. Wexford, call it a *quishin*. Chaucer had that one. 'And with that worde, he for a quishin ran. / And said knelith now whiles that thou lest.' From Latin *culcita*, a mattress.)

Abide: In Ringsend to say 'I can't abide that fellow' means 'I can't tolerate him'; but in Liverpool it also meant to put up with something, pain, for instance. (In the sense of tolerate, Shakespeare has 'I cannot abide swaggerers' in Henry IV, part 2; and in the sense of endure, he has, in Henry VI: 'What fates impose, that men must needs abide, It boot not to resist both wind and tide.' From Old English *abidan*, from *a* (intensive) plus *bidan*, to wait).

Thank you, Mrs Murphy for your words. And for the Mass card.

Gligger – Geck – Charlady – Blowze

Mrs Joan Power from Waterford sends me a brace of words re-membered from her youth. The first is *gligger*. A *gligger* is a prankster and no doubt it comes from the Old English *glig*, a jest. Variants are found in 16th-century English, and I wonder if they have travelled to this country. 'Nay, I can *gleek* upon occasion', says Bottom to Titania. *Glaiks* is an earlier variant. In Lyndesay's *Satyre* of 1535 you'll find 'I se they have playit me the glaiks.' There was, it seems, an old card game called *Gleek*, and to play the *gleek* or *glaik* meant to deceive your opponent. (I am aware of the Ulster and Scots words *gleek* and *glaik*, to glance, to stare in a rude fashion; as nouns, a peep, a talkative person, a *gligeen*. These, however, may not be related to Shakespeare's and Lyndesay's *gleek* and *glaik*.)

To Mrs Power's second word, *geck*, a dupe, a simpleton. This is an old word found in Scotland and in Ulster as *gowk*, and in places on the banks of the Barrow, as *gock*. It comes from Old Norse *gowkr*, the cuckoo. The Dutch had *gecken*, to mock. Shakespeare was fond of Mrs Power's *geck*. In *Twelfth Night* Malvolio complains to Olivia about being made 'the most notorious geck and gull that e'er invention play'd on'.

Charlady is a word that intrigues Mrs Margaret Byrne of Artane. She wonders if it is connected with *chore*. *Char*, sometimes *chare*, is an old word for drudgery. You'll find 'The maid that milks And does the meanest chares' in *Antony and Cleopatra*. Its origin is the Old English *cerr*.

Finally, an anonymous Cork teacher asks what Goldsmith meant when he wrote in *The Vicar of Wakefield* that he didn't like to see his daughters 'trudging up to their pew all *blowzed* and red with walking'. *Blowze* is a dialect word for a ruddy-faced girl. Origin unknown, the dictionaries say. Surely it's connected with *blow*, a blossom (a word that comes from the German *bluhen*, to bloom) and to the Limerick dialect word *blowen*, a good-looking young woman? I think so, for what it's worth, and I think Shakespeare is on my side. In *Titus Andronicus* he wrote: 'Sweet blowze, you are a beauteous blossom, sure ...'

To Won – Clevy – Clushet – Clavel

The verb *to won* is to be found in many places in the north of this fair isle. It means to reside, to dwell. Anne Lavery from Derry asks me where it came from.

It is an old Scots word but it is found in many of England's northern counties as well in various forms: *woane*, *wone* and *wunn* among them. Burns has 'There's auld rob Morris that wons in yon glen.' Scott, in his *Minstrelsy*, has 'I cam to see my ae brother That wons in this grene-wood.' From the verb we have the noun *wonner*, an inhabitant, and both *wonning-house*, a dwelling. Hamilton's *Outlaws* (1897), a book full of good, earthy language, has 'The byre's the place or flea-luggit auld clushets, and no the wonning-house.' This particular *clushet*, by the way, is one who is in charge of a cow-house. It probably represents *close-herd*. A clushet in Ayrshire, however, means a cow's udder: in Norfolk it means something else entirely: it is applied by women to men they don't particularly like. These clushets

[37]

come from Middle Dutch *klosse*, a bag, a testicle. But I'm rambling. As for Anne Lavery's *won*, its origin is Old English *wunian*, to dwell.

Sean Mac Conchradh of Blackrock, Co. Dublin, asks if the word *clevy* (a Munster word, we both think) is Irish in origin. It's in Irish as *cleihbí*, but the word came here from southern dialect English, a variant of *clavel*. It means, of course, a beam of wood serving as a lintel above an old-fashioned fireplace; the shelf above the fireplace, the mantlepiece. It's found all over the place from Gloucestershire south. From Old French *clavel*. Its modern French relative is *claveau*, an arch-stone.

If I may be permitted to ramble again, there is another English *clavel*. It is a mill word, also found as *clevel*, and it means a grain of corn. There was a popular belief in Kent that each clavel of wheat bore the likeness of Christ, the True Corn of Wheat. One old-timer wrote to the EDD: 'A man said to me at Eastry, "Brown wheat shows it more than white, because it's a bigger clevel. To see the likeness, the clevel must be held with the seam of the grain from you".' Has this *clavel* or *clevel* travelled to the mills of Ireland, I wonder? And has that lovely bit of English *seanchas*?

Clock – Auspicious

The little word *clock* is bothering Anne Fitzgerald from Clontarf. She asks if there is a connection between Irish *clog*, a bell, and *clog*, a clock: she also wants to know if there is a connection between the slang 'to clock', to strike, hit, and the word for the instrument that tells the time.

In the early Middle Ages words for a bell which were obviously related sprang up in the Teutonic countries as well as in those whose languages were Celtic. A bell was known since the 8th century in Merovingian Latin (used in Gaul and western Germany from 500 to 700 AD) as *clocca*: Old Irish had *cloc*; Old High German had *cloccon* and *chlocchon*; and Middle German had *klocken*, to strike, knock, which survives in Irish schoolboy slang. The early diffusion of these words was apparently connected with the diffusion of Christianity and was confined to northern and western Europe (in the southern Romantic languages the word for a bell was *campana*).

The place of origin of the various words for the northern and western bells is undetermined, but on historical considerations most scholars refer to these words as being of Celtic origin. They are echoic, imitating the noise of the early handbells which were made of sheet iron and of a quadrilateral shape; the cast-iron circular bell was of a later date. *Clock* as a word for a timepiece was introduced to England about 1300 with the Dutch striking *clocke*, probably an instrument with bells on which the hours were struck mechanically.

Auspicious is a word consistently abused by many local politicians, according to Mary White of Wexford, who says that they seem to think it means 'important'. She heard one of them say that he considered the 1798 commemoration auspicious. The word has an interesting history. The Romans foretold the future through birds. Sometimes the priest would watch their flight or observe them eating: sometimes he would examine the content of their stomachs. This process was called *auspicium*, which comes from two Latin words, *avis*, a bird, and *pecere*, to look at. (The Latin U and V were the same letter.) The *auspicia* were consulted before any great event – elections, for instance, or the departure of an army on a campaign. *Auspicium* gave *auspiciosus*, favoured by the auspices and from that the English adjective comes.

Sheldru, a Secret Language

It would appear that if you want to live long while retaining all your faculties, you should take up the study of Sheldru, the cant spoken by Irish travellers. Micheál Mac Enrí from Co. Mayo went to God at the age of 102, and Paddy Greene, the schoolmaster of Ballinalee, Co. Longford, the greatest living authority on the subject, is in his 98th year. He visited the department of Irish folklore at UCD last Christmas and in his talk showed the vitality of a man of 40.

Master Greene's contribution to the collection and study of Sheldru is acknowledged in the handsome reissue of R.A. Stewart Macalister's *The Secret Languages of Ireland*, first published in 1937, and now available in facsimile.[1] If I may refresh your memory, here are Macalister's

1 Craobh Rua Books, 12 Woodford Gardens, Armagh, £27.50 sterling including postage.

essays on Ogham, Cryptology, Hisperic, Bog-Latin, Béarlagar na Saor (the secret language of stonemasons) and the cant known variously a Shelta, Sheldru (the correct term), The Ould Thing, Minker's Tari (Tinker-speech: their term, not mine).

Kuno Meyer supported the contention that Sheldru is a secret language of great antiquity, formed on the basis of Irish at an early stage of its development. He further claimed for it a close connection, if not an identity, with the secret tongues referred to here and there in Irish literature — but you must read Macalister for an analysis of this contention. To whet your appetite here's the Lord's Prayer in Sheldru, taken down in a riverside tent from an Irish travelling man in 1890, by Dr John Sampson, the University of Liverpool's librarian. I give Sampson's word-for-word translation:

Muilsha's gather (I's father), swurth a munniath (up in goodness), munni-graua-kradyi dhuilsha munnik (good-luck-at-standing thou's name). Gra be gredhid shedhi ladhu (love be made upon earth) as aswurth I munniath (as up in goodness). Bug muilsha thalosk minurth gostha dhurra (give I day-now enough bread). Gretul our shaku (forgiveness our sin) araik muilsha getyas (like I forgives) nidyas gredhi gamiath muilsha (persons to do badness I) Nijesh solk mwi-il (not take I) sturth gamiath (into badness), but bug muilsha achim gamiath (but take I out of badness). Dhi-il the sridug (though the kingdom), thardyurath (strength) and munniath (and goodness), gradhum a gradhum (life and life).

My regards to Master Greene, Nus a Dhalyon dhuilsa, old friend.

Flotsam and Jetsam — Geld — Clink

'Here's a question for you', said an old Arklow sailor to me recently. 'Which would you prefer to find, and you walking the shoreline, flotsam or jetsam?' Not being particularly interested in either commodity, I guessed flotsam. It seems that I was right. *Flotsam* is wreckage found floating on the waves, whereas *jetsam* is that portion of the equipment or cargo of a ship thrown overboard to lighten her during a storm. There is a legal snag, however. Flotsam can be reclaimed by the ship's owners or insurers.

Two words with interesting pedigrees. *Flotsam* is from Anglo-Norman *floteson*; *flot* is compounded of Old Icelandic *flot*, floating, and the suffic -*sam*, from the Icelandic - *samr*, the equivalent of the English -*some*, in adjective that denote a quality or condition, such as *gamesome* and *winsome*.

Jetsam is a contracted form of *jettison*, the action of throwing things overboard, and that word is from Anglo-Norman *getteson*, Old French *getaison*, from Latin *jactare*, to throw.

Mary Ross was born within walking distance of the town of Sweet Strabane and she wrote to me to ask about a word used in parts of the Lagan Valley when she was young – *geld*. It is an adjective meaning barren, and the interesting thing about Mary's use of the word is that it relates only to female animals. A geld cow is one whose milk has dried up. Kelly's *Scottish Proverbs* of 1721, a book I'd like to see reprinted, has 'A geld sow was never good to grices', and was spoken to those who, having no children of their own, deal harshly with other people's. *Grice* is a young pig. It's from Old Norse *griss*. By the way, to call a pig in Kilkenny, you say *griss, griss!* Seamus Moylan's splendid book, *The Language of Kilkenny*, tells me.

The first reference to *geld*, meaning barren rather than castrated, is in *Cursor Mundi* about 1300; 'For I Sarah am geld that is me wa.' The Old Norse is *geldr*, barren, having no milk. *Gjeld* is still found in Norwegian dialect, used of a cow which for more than a year has been barren.

Finally, a man who signed his letter 'Old Lag' asked where the slang term *clink*, a prison, originates? The Clink was a jail in 16th- and 17th-century Southwark. 'He who would have been respondent must have bethought himself withal how he could refute the clink', wrote Milton in 1642.

Heugh – Let-out

The Gobbins Heughs are cliffs on the east coast of Co. Antrim, Mary Bell from Larne tells me. She requests some information about *heughs* and asks if the word *heugh* is native to Ulster.

The word came from Scotland originally, and it means, as Mary knows, I'm sure, a crag, a cliff. Burns has 'An' tho' yon lowin heugh's thy hame, Thou travels far', in his *Address to the Deil*. Scott, knowing that your average Englishman, outside of the north country, wouldn't know a heugh from cow's hock, decided to explain it in *Black Dwarf*: 'They descended the broad loaning [boreen], which winding roun the steep bank, or heugh, brought them in front of the farmhouse.' The word is alive and well in Scotland still, I'm told; to coup a person over the heugh means to ruin him.

But *heugh* has other meanings. In *Borderland Muse* (1896), a collection of verse from Northumberland I picked up long ago in Glasgow, I found the word spelled *hewe*: 'Oor wierd wild hews, Oor cairn that mem'ry still embalms, Hae nursed my muse.' EDD tells me that a hewe is a heugh, but that in the border country it means a glen, or a deep cleft in the rocks. The late John Gallagher of Dunlewey, Co. Donegal, told me that a heugh to him meant a pit, or the shaft of a coalmine. And sure enough, Wright's great dictionary quotes Graham's *Writings* (1883): 'It was mirk as in a coal heugh.'

The word is ancient. Douglas, in his *Eneados* (1513), has 'Ontill ane cave we went, Vndir a hingand (hanging) hewch.' The word is from the Old English *hah*, a promontory, literally a hanging (precipice). If you want to travel even further, take the Gothic *hah*, in *faura hah*, a hanging curtain.

Mary Kennedy from Artane has been reading Yeats's *Folk Tales*, published in 1888. She wants to know what the great man meant by the noun phrase *let-out*; his sentence was 'It was to be a great let-out entirely.' All I know is that a let-out used to mean an entertainment on a large and lavish scale, the mother and father of a hooley. I take it to be from the Irish *scaoil amach*, let out, release, set at liberty.

My Wee Naust – Glauming

A lady who wishes to remain anonymous wrote to me from Carlingford about a word her mother used and which she can't find in any dictionary. It seems that her mother, born in Scotland (my correspondent doesn't say where), purchased a cottage by the sea in Co. Down, and she would refer to it as 'my wee naust'. Is *naust* a form of nest? my friend asks.

No, but its origin is far more interesting. Also written *noust*, *noast*, and *noost*, it is a word found in fishing villages in Orkney and Shetland, and here and there across the northern coast of Scotland. It doesn't seem to have put down roots in Ulster: I would guess that the lady whose word it was brought it with her from her Scottish home.

Naust is a landing-place for boats, a slip, either natural or artificial, into which a boat is drawn up for protection against raging seas, Wright's great dialect dictionary tells me. The Carlingford woman's usage was a lovely extension of Old Norse's *naust*, a protection from storms; the word has survived in the modern Norwegian dialect word, *naust*, a boathouse. *Nest*, by the way, is from Old English *nest*, related to Latin *nidus* and to Irish *nead*.

Pádraig Ó Cíobháin, of An Spidéal, heard the word *glauming* from his mother-in-law, Kathleen Lanigan, in Kilkenny. The good lady offered this gloss: 'She'd be going around the house glauming for something – searching for something.' Pádraig notes that Peig Sayers had *ag gliúmáil*, and that Dinneen explains this as the act of peering, prying, groping. Are *glauming* and *gliúmáil* related, he wonders.

Let's take *glauming* first. It is found all over Scotland and Ireland. The verb was glossed in the EDD as 'to take hold of a woman indecorously'. An Argyle correspondent wrote that 'the verb denotes a feeble and ineffectual attempt, as that of an infant or of one groping from blindness in the dark'. This verb is of unknown origin. It's in Irish as *glám* and in Scots Gaelic as *glàm*. Is *gliúmáil*, prying, groping, related to these? God only knows.

There is also a *glaum* which means to peer. This is a different word and is of Scandinavian origin. Compare the Norwegian dialect word *glaama*, to stare.

As to *gliúmáil*, to peer, I think this is from English and Scots dialect *gloom*, to stare, related to Norwegian *glyma*, to stare, to look stern.

The Borey Dancers – Swift's Words

Nuala Ní Dhomhnaill has two splendid poems in the 1998 edition of *Irisleabhar Mhá Nuad* about the Aurora Borealis. In a fascinating introduction to the poems she tells of speaking to the Kerry folklorist, Dr Joe Daly, about local words for the phenomenon.

She herself had heard *An Chaor Aduaidh*, the northern flare. Dr Daly told her that the usual term used by the people in his young days was *The Borey Dancers*. A lovely conceit this is, as the poet says: the image of the multicoloured curtains sweeping across the sky like a group of dancers. It is indeed, and she might be interested to know that in Orkney they have a similar conceit, and a very old one too. In Wallace's *Description of the Orkney Islands*, written in 1693, I came across this: 'The North Light is, by reason of its desultory motion, called Morrice Dancers.' Poetic peoples think alike.

My colleague in University College, Dublin, the late Alan Bliss, some twenty years ago published an edition of Swift's *Dialogue in Hybernian Stile*, written about 1735. I have just finished reading it again; it is important because apart from the evidence contained in it and in Swift's other work, *Irish Eloquence*, nothing is known of the language spoken by the planters at this period. Swift showed that their English had sub-standard and dialectal features, and that it had been strongly influenced by Irish. Consider these: 'Them apples is very good'; 'I am again you in that': 'Lord, I was so boddered the other day with that prating fool Tom!' (*boddered*, deafened; compare Irish *bodhar*); 'Pray, how does he get his health?' (Remember Raftery's *má fhaghaimse sláinte* ...?); 'He's often very unwell' ('unwell' was first introduced to England by Lord Chesterfield in 1785. Said he: 'I am what you call in Ireland, and a very good expression it is, unwell'); 'Why, sometimes sowins (Irish *súghán*, flummery) and in summer we have the best frawhawns (Irish *fraocháin*, bilberries) in all the country'; 'Why, he's a meer buddough (Irish *bodach*, churl). He sometimes coshers with me (lodges, Irish *coisir*, banquet), and once a month I take a pipe with him and we shoh (take every second turn, Irish *seach*) it about for an hour together'; 'I have seen him riding on a sougane' (*súgán*, here a straw saddle); 'He is no better than a spawlpeen (*spailpín*, itinerant labourer), a perfect Monaghan' (a clown; Dr Swift didn't elaborate).

Sneck – Snib – Famble

It's a long time since I heard the word *sneck*, a latch. *Sneck* is a northern word, imported from either Scotland or northern England. Stevenson used it in *Catriona*, and it was recorded in Patterson's glossary of Antrim and Down words at the end of the last century. John Scott sent me the word from Ballyclare.

There were some interesting compounds. A *sneckdrawer* is an intruder, or an unwelcome visitor. A contributor to the EDD, a native of Fife, explained: 'When a neighbour slipped in for a crack there was some art in introducing himself to the household, so much so that a wily pawky flatterer was known familiarly as an auld sneckdrawer.'

A *snecklifter* was both an intruder and the price of a cheap drink, to allow a sponger to get initiated into a public house. In Cumbria, when a horse was tied up outside a pub it was said to eat *sneck-hay*. 'To put a sneck before his snout' meant to shut the door on an unwelcome guest. The word is found in the 15th century as *snekk*, and is of uncertain origin.

I have seen *snibs* on many's the farmhouse kitchen door in Ulster. This is how the EDD describes it. 'The snib is a small piece of wood by inserting which into the look the sneck becomes fast and cannot be raised from the outside.' I've also heard the ordinary sliding bolt referred to as a *snib* in Donegal, and not long ago I heard a young woman remind her boyfriend to *snib* the car door after he had parked it outside Sweeney's hotel in Dungloe.

I suppose the word is related to *snib* meaning to check, restrain; if I'm right the word has a Scandinavian origin. Compare Middle Swedish *snybba*, which also meant to rebuke. This is what Chaucer had in mind when he wrote: 'Him wold he snibben sharply for the nones.'

A.J. Newcombe, a native of York now residing in Dublin, wrote about the word *famble*, which means to stutter, to speak unintelligibly. The EDD says that this is also of Scandinavian origin, which won't surprise a Yorkshireman. There is, for instance, the Danish *famle*, to stammer.

P.J. Nolan of Carrowbloughmore House, Kilkee, sent me a quotation from the *Clare Journal* of 25 February 1889: ' ... the pliant tool of Norbury, Vandaleur and the perjured pimping fillibadanda ...' Can anybody help him with the f-word. I can't, I'm afraid.

Let – Bread and Tay Boys

A correspondent from Macroom who signs her letter 'Múinteoir Scoile' asks about the origin of a *let* in tennis. *Let* is an archaic noun meaning an obstruction, hindrance, stoppage. In tennis, needless to say, it means an interference with the ball; the point must be played again. Spenser has: 'Scorning the let of so unequal foe' in *The Faerie Queene*.

Shakespeare also has the noun. In *Henry V* he wrote, 'My speech entreats That I may know the let, why gentle peace Should not expel these inconveniences.' The noun has survived down to our time in the phrase 'let or hindrance'. From Old English *lettan*, to hinder. It is related to late – *laet* meant slow.

The archaic verb *let*, to hinder, prevent, is found in Chaucer's *Tale of the Man of Lawe*: 'The day goth faste, I wol no lenger lette.' You'll remember 'Unhand me, gentlemen – By heaven, I'll make a ghost of him that lets me', from *Hamlet*.

Joan Pender, a Kilkenny woman who now lives in Artane, writes to remind me of the insulting term *bread and tay boys* used by the followers of the country hurling teams in taunting teams from the towns at matches in the 1950s.

She adds a few more: the *coffee an' crames*, the *butterflies*, the *after you, Margarets*. It was ever thus, Joan. The Cockneys in Tudor times were known as the *toast-and-butters*, one of my sons tells me. Beaumont and Fletcher in *Wit without Money* have: 'They love young toasts and butter, Bow Bell suckers'. The term was here used of effeminate men.

Of cowards Falstaff spoke in *Henry IV*: 'I pressed me none but such toasts and butter, with hearts in their bellies no bigger than pins' heads.'

Never one to put a *sper* on their tongues, those Tudors. *Sper* is John McDonagh's word; John is a Galwayman who now lives in London's Hampstead. This is the Irish *speir*, a fetter; a leg fetter for sheep, according to Father Dinneen. A borrowing from English, this, I feel sure. Spenser has 'Sperre the gate fast for fear of fraude' in *The Shepherd's Calendar*. Shakespeare has: 'With massy staples and corresponsive

[46]

and fulfilling bolts Sperr up the sons of Troy' in one of my favourite plays, *Troilus and Cressida*. The Old English was *sparian*, to fasten with a bolt.

Bastable – Stillion – Wig

May I thank the many people who wrote to tell me that the Cork word, *bastable*, a pot oven, got its name from the Devonshire town in which these utensils were first made, Barnstaple. Seeing that Jurgen Küllman from Dortmund was the first to let me know, to him goes the lollipop.

An interesting letter from Paul Harries of Canterbury, a teacher of English: 'I read with great interest your gloss on *stellan, stillion*, etc. You'll know the passage in *King Lear*. "The sea, with such a storm as his bare head in hell-black night endured, would have buoy'd up, and quench'd the stelled fires." For many years I have been repeating to my students the received explanation of *stelled* as being one of Shakespeare's coinages, a contraction for *stellated*, from Latin *stella*.

'How wrong so many of the commentators are in this! It is now clear to me that *stelled* is from the same source as your *stellan*, Old English *stellan*, to set, place; and that what the great man meant when he wrote stelled fires was fixed stars.'

I'd accept that. I note that Shakespeare also has: 'Mine eye hath play'd the painter and hath stelled Thy beauty's form in table of my heart' in Sonnet 24. Full marks, Mr Harries.

Ciarán Ó Muirí of Anner Road, Inchicore, was having a jar with some men in a Coolock pub recently. One of them remarked that he would rather drink in a hotel. This, Ciaran tells me, was greeted with laughter, and somebody said that your man only went there because of the *wiggers*. The word meant women, he was told.

A fine old word this, related to the verb *wig*, to waggle, shake, and also to wiggle. The word is in English since the 13th century when it was imported from Middle Low German or Middle Dutch *wiggelen*. By 1900 it was confined to Shetland, according to the EDD, which had never heard of Coolock and its wigging pieces.

Piece is a word used almost exclusively in contempt of a woman

[47]

by other women in the area around Clonmel, according to a medical doctor who knows which side his bread is buttered on and so desires anonymity. Old slang this, and common. Shakespeare has it in *Titus Andronicus*: 'Go, give that changing piece to him that flourish'd for her with his sword.' The speaker was male, however: Saturninus, a wigger fancier who never gave much thought to political correctness, sensible man.

Grumpy as a Hare — A Boy or a Child — Hothouse Flowers

Lady Macbeth's 'poor cat i' th' adage' is troubling John Murphy of the City of the Cats, as he calls Kilkenny. What is the adage the good lady was speaking about when she chides her husband for 'letting "I dare not" wait upon "I would" ', he asks. She was alluding, John, to: 'The cat loves fish but dares not wet his feet!'

We'll stay with the Tudors. An old man who lives in my part of Co. Wicklow was recently described by his daughter as 'grumpy as a hare'. Strange, isn't it, how the hares are considered to be out of sorts, except, of course, when they go slightly mad in March and can be seen coup-carleying in the moonlight.

The notion that the hare is melancholy is a very old one. When Falstaff complains to the young prince that he is as melancholy as a gib cat, a lugg'd bear and the drone of a Lincolnshire bagpipe, the prince says: 'What sayest thou to a hare, or the melancholy of Moorditch?'

Turberville, in his *Book on Hunting and Falconry*, was the first to attempt an explanation for the sprightly animal's disposition: 'The hare first taught us the use of the hearbe called Wylde Succory, which is very excellent for those which are disposed to melancholicke: shee herself is one of the most melancholicke beasts that is, and to heal her owne infirmitie shee goeth commonly to sit under the herbe.'

Dr Johnson remarked: 'A hare may be considered as melancholy because she is upon her form solitary; and according to the physic of the times, the flesh of it was supposed to generate melancholy.' And when Lady Answerall, in Swift's *Polite Conversation*, was asked to eat hare, she refused saying, 'No, madam, they say 'tis melancholy meat.'

I think it's fairly well known that in some parts of Ireland - and in southern England too - a female infant is called a child. Hence the question: 'Is it a boy or a child?' Here we have another Tudor relic. In *The Winter's Tale* the old shepherd says: 'Mercy on's, a barne: a very pretty barne! a boy or a child, I wonder?'

And I wonder does Mr Ó Maonlaí know that *Hothouse Flowers* was a Tudor euphemism for ladies who worked in houses of ill-repute? Steam baths were one of the amenities: so Ben Jonson tells us in *Every Man Out of His Humour.*

Stillan — Fecket — Hoity-toity

I am grateful to many readers for informing me that Billy Colfer's Slade word, *stellin(g)* is found in many places in various disguises. Madge Anderson, of Trees Road, Mount Merrion, Dublin, remembers her mother's *stillion*, a timber bench or form, pronounced *furrum* (Irish *fuarma*). 'On it stood the milk churns to be sent to the creamery the following day.'

The Revd James Brennan, of Kilkenny, says that he well remembers the *stillan* in his grandmother's house in Graine, Urlingford. 'It was a cold room with shelves on which large pans of milk were kept, as were buckets of water and anything that had to be kept cool.'

Thanks to those who wrote to remind me that Irish has borrowed the word as *stillín*, especially to a wretch who signed her letter Martina.

'I'm worried about you', she says, 'You need to eat more fish and to down a few more taoscáns every night. Your brain needs nurture and lubrication. You explained this word *stillín* to us in UCD in the 1980s, you know, and told us that it came from *stell*, with *ing* added to make a noun of it, just as you told Mr Colfer.'

James Hannon, from Larne, asks about the word *fecket*. It is a word he has heard many times in Scotland. Fecket is a vest, or a *simmet*, to use the Ulster word.

Burns had: 'Grim loon! He gat me by the fecket' in his *Poem to Mr Mitchel*. A *fir fecket* was, and probably still is, a coffin in Burns country. Origin unknown.

Fecket has not, apparently, been recorded in Ulster. *Simmet* is very common. This seems to be used only of a man's vest, or a baby's. A Scots word, it may have come directly from Old French *samit*, a silk undergarment.

Another French import that has since travelled the world from Scotland is *caddie*. From *cadet*, the youngest son, caddies were once sent by the noble families of Scotland to serve as attendants in other great houses.

The lady who wrote this never played golf: 'Where will I get a little foot-page, Where will I get a caddie. That will run swift to bonnie Aboyne, Wi a letter to my rantin' laddie?'

Thanks to Deansún Breatnach, of Dún Laoghaire, for his suggestion that *hoity-toity*, as well as the Scots and Ulster word *howtowdy*, may be traced to Old French *huteaudeau*, a pullet.

Whipster – Rouse

There are so many allegations of skulduggery being levelled at the moment at so many of our beloved policasters that I consider the word I heard used by an old Wicklow lady the other night as rather mild. 'A proper whipster, that fellow', she said.

Whipster is an old word. It means a doubtful character, an untrustworthy fellow. It echoes the origins of *whip*, Middle Dutch and Middle Low German *wippen*, to move up and down, to oscillate, to swing. The *-ster* bit is from Middle English *-estre*, Old English *-istre*, *-estre*, a feminine suffix. There is then an indication of contemptuous inferiority implied in my Wicklow lady's feminine termination just as there was in Shakespeare's 'Every puny whipster gets my sword.' *Othello*, children. In Donegal, and perhaps in other places in Ireland as well, a *whipster* is what a Dubliner would call a *rozzie*, a romping girl, according to Simmons's Donegal glossary of 1890.

John Burke, a Galwayman writing from Long Island, New York, sent me a word I haven't heard in years, *rouse*, which means a drinking bout. John asks why the word is attenuated: he, like myself, thought it a variant of *carouse*. It's not, apparently. When John writes, 'He was on a ferocious rouse in Ballinasloe,' I take it that he heard the word at home and not in America.

Carouse is from German (*trinken*) *gar aus*, (to drink) right out. John's *rouse* is related to the Swedish *rus*, a drinking bout. They also have *rusa*, to fuddle. That the word is Scandinavian may also be suspected from this passage in Dekker's *The Gulls Hornbook* (1609): 'Tell me then soveraigne skinker, how to take the German's upsy-freeze, the Danish rowsa, the Switzer's stoop to Rheinish.' You won't be surprised that Master Shakespeare also knew the word. He has 'The King's rouse the heavens shall bruit again' in *Hamlet*. In *Othello* we find 'They have given me a rouse already': here *rouse* meant a bumper, a large measure.

Can anybody help with two words sent to my by Gerry McCarthy of Botanic Road, Glasnevin?: *cohallion* and *coheemer*. 'The reference was always to elderly gentlemen who would qualify for the description loveable, grámhar', says my correspondent. East Waterford words these.

Motions – Peat – Stickler

The old lady in the West Cork pub was annoyed. The young one who passed by on her way to powder her nose wore a dress that would have got her arrested in Mykonos. 'Has she any idea what she can to do a man's motions in that outfit?' said Hannah to me. 'So this is what Irish girlhood, once a shining light in a pagan world, has come to!' 'A sad day for Ireland, surely Hannah', her husband agreed. I wondered why they both assumed that *my* motions were unlikely to be affected by the girl who had forgotten to put on her underwear. *Motions* is a Cork word. Its origin is the Latin *motio*, a moving, from *movere*, to move. Of course it's related to *emotion*, both words coming our way from *movere*; *emotion*, however, by way of Old French *esmovoir*, to excite, from Latin *emovere*, to disturb. There is a striking line in a 19th-century macaronic song from Cork called *The Girl from the Mill*. A young scamp has enticed her into a pub and, he tells us: 'We fell to drinking Beamish's porter to coax her motions in high display.' You'll be relieved to know that he failed; her mother appeared.

Motion in this sense of carnal impulse was known to a rather better poet than our Cork balladeer. He has it in *Othello*, where Iago says: 'We have reason to cool our raging motions, our carnal stings, our unbitted lusts.'

Peat is a word sent to me by Julia Shaw from Cultra, Co. Down. It means a spoiled young woman. Scott has it in *Heart of Midlothian*: 'Ye are baith a pair o' the devil's peats, I trow.' Massinger has it in *The Maid of Honour* : 'Of a little thing, You are a pretty peat, indifferent fair too.' Shakespeare used the word just once, in *The Taming of the Shrew*. John Foster's glosses on Tudor words says that it's from French *petit*. I have never come across the word in Ireland.

'A stickler for rules': P. Hennessy from Carlow wants to know the origin of *stickler*. It's from the obsolete *stightle*, to rule, regulate. Oxford links it to Old English *stightan*, *stightian*. A stickler was an umpire or referee in medieval trials of honour. The word is found in Shakespeare's *Troilus and Cressida*: 'The dragon wing of night o'erspreads the earth, and stickler-like, the armies separates.'

Breó – Doornick – Smool

I see that Guinness is about to introduce a new beer called *Breó*, a name decided upon 'after some consultation with Bord na Gaeilge and a number of fluent Irish speakers', according to a report published recently in this paper. It is to spend £5 million marketing the product. I wish it well. '*Breó*, pronounced Bro [it isn't, darlings], is a Celtic word meaning glow', we were informed, and the name was chosen 'as it reflects the original attributes, colour and look of the product'.

Breó (also *bréo*, monosyllable and *breö*, disyllable), a flame, a blaze, is an Irish word of unknown origin, used extensively of saints and heroes in our early literature in a complimentary sense: *Patriaicc ... breö batses genti*: Patrick, a flame that baptised the heathen; *A Stefan, a breó náob*, O Stephen, holy fire. *Breo-shaighead*, arrow of flame, is a later conventional metaphoric name for Brigid – a *kenning* is what the scholars say, Joxer, an Old Icelandic word meaning a mark of recognition, from *kenna vith*, to name after. *Breóad*, earlier *brëud*, was the act of burning, injuring: and, according to my friend Father Dinneen, *breo* also meant 'a fire that proceeds from putrid matter, as fish, etc.' and also the act of getting sick and enfeebled. I wonder did Uncle Arthur and his fluent advisers take this into account as they cogitated?

Seán Ó Briain, of Clonmel and of RTÉ Radio's once splendid drama department, gave me the word *doornick* recently. Last night I herd the word again, when a young lady, dressed as William Morris might have dressed her, entered a Wicklow hostelry in a *breó* of loveliness. *Doornick* to Seán Ó Briain was a coarse damask formerly used to make altar cloths and ecclesiastical hangings: old-timers who live between the Willow Grove and Roundwood call richly decorated clothes *doornicks*. The word is from *Doornik*, the Flemish name of Tournai, the Belgian town famous for its carpets and tapestry work.

Lastly an interesting trawler-man's word, sent to me by Tom Carr from Killybegs. 'He ate the whole loaf of bread when he came in from the pub. Not a *smool* did he leave us for the breakfast.' Is *smool* Irish, my correspondent asks?

It is of Norse origin and is found as *smuil*, *smill* and *smyle* in northern Scotland and in Orkney, and as *smjill* in Shetland. Compare the Swedish *smule*, a crumb.

Jildy – Mingin – Gossamer – Cavan Saucepans

Christmas time stirs fond memories of old words, Tom Mullins of King Street, Mitchelstown, remember his father's strange word *jildy* or *gildy* – he's never seen it spelled. It is, or was, an adjective used on the Limerick side of the Galtee mountains instead of neat, smart, tidy. One would say: 'Isn't that a jildy dress?'

All I can offer here is a guess. There is an old Norse word, *gildr*, an adjective defined by Vigfusson's dictionary as 'of full worth, of full size, complete, stout'.

A Norse word surviving in the foothills of the Galtees? Stranger things have happened.

Geraldine Monaghan of Parnell Road, Dolphin's Barn, heard the word *mingin* from a northern friend. The word means dirty, stinking.

This word is common in the north: I've heard it myself in Donegal. It came from Scotland, where *ming*, verb, means to mix. The mix referred to was a concoction of human excrement, urine and other dainties used in the treatment of fleeces: from Old English *mingan*, to mix.

A rare beauty came from somebody who signed his letter 'Bannow Rambler'. He heard it from a man who used to hunt with the Wexford hounds many years ago.

Gossamer we all know to be a gauze of silk fabric of the very finest texture; also a filmy cobweb often seen on foliage. But the huntsman's gossamer was that misty vapour that rises from winter fields as the morning sun strikes them, a portent of a good hunting scent.

All gossamers are from *gos*, goose, plus *somer*, summer, and refers to St Martin's Summer round Armistice Day, or yours truly's birthday, whichever you prefer, when it was traditional to eat goose. Look at the morning hedgerows at that time of the year and you'll notice the prevalence of cobwebs.

Christmas prompted Jack Foley of Corebeagh, Cootehill, Co. Cavan, to tell me that saucepans to the women cooking the Christmas, as was said, were simply mugs of various sizes: what you or I would call a saucepan was called a burner.

Finally, reminded by the many letters received about Barney Cavanagh's *gowpen*, the full of two cupped hands, may I echo the Scots poet Hogg, who 200 years ago this Christmas asked the Virgin to fling doun frae her lap *gowpens* of benedicities on his readers. Go n-eirí an Nollaig libh.

Dead as Doornails — Black Monday — Sod

A man who has been reading Anthony Cronin's *Dead as Doornails* writes to ask where the phrase had its origin. Let me quote the great

Steevens on the matter. He wrote, over a century ago now: 'This proverbial expression is oftener used than understood. The door nail is the nail on which in ancient doors the knocker strikes. It is therefore used as a comparison to any one irrecoverably dead, one who has fallen (as Virgil says) *multa morte*, that is, with abundant death, such as iteration of strokes on the head would naturally produce.' There you are, Mr Kelly.

From 'Waterford Woman' comes a letter asking me about Black Monday. There was a fairly recent Black Monday, she vaguely remembers – something to do with a stock-market collapse, she thinks – but, she asks, wasn't there a calamity of some kind long ago which gave rise to the name?

Indeed there was. It was Easter Monday, 14 April 1360, and it was called Black because of the severity of the day. The soldiers of Edward III, standing around Paris when they should have stood at home, froze to death. Shakespeare mentions it in *The Merchant of Venice*: 'It was not for nothing that my nose fell a-bleeding on Black Monday last.'

An interesting question from a Dublin lady who knows her Bible better than I do. She quotes Genesis and asks about the word *sod* in 'And Jacob sod porridge.' It's the past participle of *seethe*, of which it should more correctly be the preterite. Here it means boiled. Shakespeare talks of 'twice-sod simplicity' in *Love's Labour's Lost*: he means twice boiled down, hence, concentrated. In Tudor times to sod had also come to mean to steep, to bathe. 'Her eyes, though sod in tears, look'd red and raw' is from *The Rape of Lucrece*.

Far from the Bible were my thoughts as another sod came to what's left of my mind recently as I watched Tom Kilroy's play in the Abbey. That other sod, noun and verb, is as all the world knows, from sodomy, but what brought a smile to my eyes was not the abbreviation, traced by Partridge to the British navy *c.*1818, but rather Swinburne's quatrain about poor, dear Oscar. It's rather good, don't you think?

When, Oscar came to join his God,
Not earth to death, but sod to sod,
It was for sinners such as this
Hell was created bottomless.

Beholding – Words from Newfoundland

A lady from Bray is annoyed about the recent acquisition of the DART* accent by her daughter. When the girl's mother is not in she's *ite*, and the deathtrap at Loughlinstown Hospital is known to her as *rindabite*. And worse, says my correspondent, she says *I'm beholding to you*.

Hold hard there, missus. I'm with you all the way about the DART speak, but *beholding* is a venerable old word. Yes, I suppose it started life as a spelling error, when used instead of the past participle *beholden*, obliged. But somebody very literate indeed put the stamp of authority on the corrupted spelling, or grammatical error, or whatever, a long time ago. I came across this: 'I am beholding to you for your sweet music this last night.' No, not an actress bidding good morrow to a bishop, but Simonides talking to Pericles in Shakespeare's play.

In all probability the Bray lassie is merely being genteel in saying *beholding*, but the dialect dictionaries tell me the word is alive and well across the water, from Leicestershire to Somerset, where they also have the lovely noun, *beholdingness*, obligation.

Dr Vincent McMahon practises the healing art in Carbonear, Newfoundland. He has sent me a few words he overheard in his surgery recently. A woman described her husband as a *crackawley*. This is the Irish *craiceálaí*, from English dialect *cracked*, mad. Like the vast number of words of Irish origin one finds in Newfoundland English, it must have come with the cod fishermen of the south east two centuries ago, many of whom found life easier in Talamh an Eisc, the Fishing Ground. Strange that Dineen doesn't have the word. Ó Dónaill does.

The language of Newfoundland has its charming old euphemisms. 'I am a victim of the costive bowel', elderly patients have told Dr McMahon, when they meant they were constipated. And some old plurals have survived, either from south-east Wexford English or from the dialects of southern England. A man complained of having *six nestes of waspes* near his house. They used to have *dugges and caudes* south of Rosslare, not dogs and cats. An old man from Carne once told me that he had burned a new pair of *shoon* in the *ashen*. Chaucer

*Dublin Area Rapid Transit

[56]

wouldn't have raised an eyebrow. Neither, I fancy, would some of Vincent McMahon's patients. I am beholding to him.

Omelette – Jumper – Munchie – Staughy

Many of the words connected with food have interesting pedigrees. Take *omelette*. It came to us in the 17th century from the French *omelette*, changed from *alumette*, from *alumelle*, the blade of a sword. This *alumelle*, in its turn, was changed by mistaken division from *la lamelle*, from Latin *lamella*, diminutive of *lamina*, a thin plate of metal. The omelette, then, was so called because of its thin, flat shape: and the French, in making a hash of things, gave English a beautiful word.

Nancy Reich, from Orlando, Florida, bought a *báinín* jumper recently. She knows where *báinín* comes from, thanks to an Internet friend in Bord Failte: it's the *jumper* can be traced back to the Arabic *jubbah*, a long loose linen coat adopted by the Crusaders from the Saracens. By the 17th century the word had become *jump*, and it was chiefly used of a short coat worn by Presbyterian ministers. A century later, Dr Johnson defines it as 'a waistcoat: a kind of loose and limber stays worn by sickly ladies'.

The longer word *jumper* first appeared in 1852: it was a garment worn by sailors, and did not become fashionable until this century, when women decided that it looked quite well on them too, especially when worn nice and tight.

Two small queries from C.J. Slator of Hawthornden Road, Belfast. When he was a small boy and came home with his socks down over his boots, his grandmother used to say, 'You're like an old munchie.' *Munchie*, common enough in placenames in the north, is the Irish *móinteach*, mossland, moorland. She was calling young Master Slator a bogman.

His second word is *staughy*, not found in the dictionaries and thus important as well as being elusive. *Staughy* is a mixture of leftovers: 'Are we having a staughy for tea tonight?' This, I'm pretty sure, is from the Irish *stác*, defined by O'Reilly's dictionary as offal.

Clue – Panic – Marriage over the Tongs

If you are given to reading 19th-century fiction, as Ann Crankshaw of Bangor is, you'll have noticed that detectives, suspicious husbands and the like, snooped around looking for clews. Ann wants to know if clew is simply a variant spelling of clue, and would like to know a little about its history.

Well, I suppose one should say that clue is a variant spelling of clew, because the latter is much older. When it first appeared in English it meant a ball (Old High German *kliu*) and soon it had the sense 'a ball of thread'. But as to the origin of the use of the word to mean something that enables one to solve a mystery, it can be traced to the story of Theseus, who went forth to kill the Minotaur, the monster who lived in the centre of the labyrinth of Crete.

Theseus would not have got very far without the help of the king's daughter, Ariadne, who gave him a ball of thread to unwind a he went into the labyrinth, so that he'd be able to find his way back again. This, it is said, is how *clue* came to mean something that helps one to penetrate the labyrinth of a mystery.

A friend who teaches in north London tells me that the latest in-word in the English of West Indian immigrant children is *panic*. 'The black Spice Girl is panic, man': somebody very sexy.

Well, it's good to know that the memory of the Greek god of nature is kept dimly alive in the school playgrounds of Brent. Pan, you may remember, had the rather nasty habit of making scary noises in lonesome places in the dead of night, and came to be regarded as the cause of sudden fright or groundless terror. *Panicos* is a Greek adjective meaning connected with or under the influence of Pan: when the English borrowed the word they discarded the termination.

To the dusky lady. My friend asked his pupils how exactly she scared them. 'She don't make you panic, teacher: she make you *exciteed*, man. She is miserable [mischievous to us]. She *is* panic.' Their very own superlative, not in their parents' vocabulary – yet.

Wicked – Orchestra – Caper

I am told by the London teacher who sent me the West Indian school word *panic*, sexually exciting, that *wicked* is another word they have converted to their use. To them a wicked person is good, not evil, and with a touch of magic about him or her.

Their use of wicked is interesting. The masculine of witch is the Old English *wicca* which comes from *wiccian*, to bewitch. From *wiccian* comes *wicked*, a word which once upon a time meant addicted to witchcraft. So, is the West Indian kid who calls his hero, Andy Cole, wicked, all that much offside?

Jack Hennessy from Waterford wrote to remind me of the days of our youth when a dance band, even when it played in rural halls lit by oil lamps, was called an orchestra. The difference between an orchestra and a band seemed to be that the former wore formal dress, and was conducted by a man who held a baton in a white-gloved hand while facing the dancers, not his musicians. Jack, like myself, remembers a Waterford maestro conducting his orchestra, the late edition of the *Evening Mail* on the podium in front of him in place of a score. Anyway, the word orchestra intrigues my nostalgic friend.

The Greek *orchos* meant a row of fruit trees. It is not related to *orchard*, as you might imagine. From a row of trees it was applied to a row of dancers, then to the semi-circular area in front of the stage where the chorus performed their ritual dances. Nowadays musicians, not dancers, sit in front of the stage if their services are needed: and so it came to be that we called a band by a name that was, long long ago, associated with dancers, who capered in their ritual routines.

Ah yes, and what capers we ourselves had! *Caper*, by the way, is the Latin for a goat. A wild goat was called *capreolus*, from which the French made *cabriole*, a buck-leap, if you will, and afterwards, *cabriolet*, a springy two-wheeled carriage. Too long by far for the English and the Yanks, they shortened the French word to *cab*.

Oh dear, look how far I've rambled from Mr Hennessy's rural halls: dark, smoky, wicked places – wicked in the West Indian sense. I still vividly remember those white gloves waving in the light of dim lamps above the capering throng, like lilies in hell ...

Pattern – Grammar

'I have often wondered', writes Margaret Gladney from Hollybush Road, Liverpool, 'why Irish people pronounce the word "patron" *pattern*. In the part of Ireland I come from, south Carlow, people always refer to the Pattern of St Mullins: why is this so?'

Father is a very ancient word indeed and is found in all the Aryan languages in various forms, the Greek and Latin *pater* among them. From *pater* came the Latin *patronus*, a person in a father-like position, such as the master of a freed slave or a lord who is looked to for protection. To the early Christians it was the name attached to a saint to which a religious community or indeed an individual person was dedicated. Saints were, of coure, models to be imitated and patron came to mean model. In the 16th century, patron acquired the pronunciation pattern, and became a fair in honour of a patron saint. The pronunciation has since been peculiar to Ireland, the exception being Wexford's barony of Forth, where Lady's Island pattern, Ilone Vaar (Island Fair), continued to be called a *patroon*, due to their French connection, until the end of the last century.

It may surprise you to learn that most of our university students know precious little about grammar. Grammar is descended from Greek *grammatike*, from *gramma*, a letter as a division mark (think of 'Section A') from *graphein*, to write. Grammar formerly meant, not the scientific study of classes, sounds and forms of words in a language but learning in general. In the dark ages when learned men were thought to be in league with the powers of darkness, grammar began to be used in a general sense as a word for magic.

The Scots, probably cogging from the Old French *gramaire*, magic, had *gramaire* and *gramery*. Would your friendly publican, if you echoed the gent in the Towneley Mystery of 1450 and said, just after he called Time for the tenth time, 'Cowthe ye by your gramery reche us a drynk?' pull another pint for you? The Scots had another related word for enchantment, *glamour*.

Walter Scott may take the credit for introducing the word into standard English: but the word is still used in the north of Ireland as the *Ballymena Observer* recorded it in 1890: 'After Hallow Eve the divil throws his *glammery* over the blackberries.' And that, Mary Smith of Drummin, Co. Longford, is where glamour came from.

A Soft Day – Moy – Jundie – Hogshouter

I once heard an American academic say at a Summer school that the expression *a soft day* was a testimony to the genius of the Irish race. It was, he explained, a translation from the Irish *lá bog*, and that we kept this treasure in our speech when our own sublime language was stolen from us by the Sasanachs, blah, blah, blah. Many Scots and English people would be surprised at his theory. Wright's great dictionary tells us that 'soft day!' is a common greeting in Cornwall; that 'it's a soft Spring day' was recorded where Shakespeare went to school; that 'the weather fell round to soft' was heard in Devon; and that all over the north country, people say things like 'That's a nice soft day, thanks be to God'.

In Scotland, Scott has 'A fine soft morning for the crap, sir'. In case you might think that sir was caught unawares behind a gorse bush on his grouse moor, *crap* is Scots for *crop*.

'That's a *moy* day', a Yorkshire friend said to me recently. Found in the north of England and in Scotland, *moy* in older Scots meant gentle, mild, soft. Used of people it meant reserved, but by 1715 it had come to mean affecting great moderation in eating or drinking. Kelly, in his (Scottish) *Proverbs* of 1721 has: 'A bit butt and bit bend make a moy maiden at the board's end.' This was a reflection on young women who didn't eat much at dinner, intimating that if they hadn't been raiding the pantry they wouldn't leave their food behind them at table. *Butt* is a Scots word for a buttock of beef. Norwegian and Swedish dialects have *butt*, a little stump, a mouthful. *Bend* was a slang word for a draught of liquor; the verb meant to drink hard. Hence *bender*, a drinker, and *to go on a bender*. Anyway, *moy* is from French *mou*, *mol*, from Latin *mollis*: of weather, mild; of character, tender, sensitive; of gradients, easy; of speech, tender, moving.

A man from Glenarm sent me the word *jundie*, a word unknown in the south, I'd say. It means to jostle, to shoulder. A Scots word this. Burns has it: 'The warly race may drudge and drive, Hogshouther, jundie, stretch an' strive.' *Hogshouther* was a game in which players shoulder-charged the opposition to up-end them. Fuitball without the ball.

Havoc – Lords and Princesses

The Norsemen of old never got a good press anywhere they went. No doubt about it, they were hard chaws, and it is generally accepted nowadays that they gave us the word *havoc*, as is found in the expression 'to cry havoc', which intrigues Mary Dunphy from Kilkenny. The word was introduced into French as *havot*, and into late Latin as *havo*. The Anglo-Normans spelled it *havok*. The origin of the word is obscure but it is first found in the Viking strongholds of northern France as a word of command to a band of raiders giving them the go-ahead to pillage to their hearts' content. Oh, they were rough men, all right, but as Fergus Kelly shows in his wonderful new book, *Early Irish Farming*,* a work which can be thoroughly enjoyed by non-specialists, Ireland of the Welcomes didn't always greet them with cries of *fáilte!* when they came ashore from their longboats. The Annals of Ulster for 1013 tell us that one King Gilla Mo-Chonna of Southern Brega captured a band of them, and having yoked most of them to a plough, forced others to follow, harrowing from their scrotums.

The word *lord* the Anglo Saxons gave us: *prince* came by way of the Romans, and the *-ess* in *princess* came from France, by way of Rome and Greece. Mary Clune from Limerick was asking.

Lord, like his Lady, takes his name from bread. In the early Anglo-Saxon household a servant was called *hlaf-aeta*, eater of the master's bread: *hlaf*, which became our loaf, being the Anglo Saxon for bread. The master who supplied the bread was called *hlaf-weard* (half+ward, ward being a keeper). After a while the word was written as *hlaford*, and it eventually reached us as *lord*. Lady is from Old English *hlaefdige*, from *hlaf+dig*, knead.

From *primus*, first, and *capere*, to take, the Romans made *princeps*, the man who takes first. *Princeps* became a favoured title after the Civil Wars which left Octavianus Caesar as top cat. He was afraid to offend people by calling himself King, but he enjoyed so much power that *princeps* inevitably came to mean a royal person. The English merely shortened the Latin word later on.

The *-ess* in princess is from Old French *-essa*, denoting a female person or animal, from Late Latin - *issa*, from Greek *-issa*.

*Dublin Institute for Advanced Studies, 750 pp, £16 hardback.

Tinsel – Cot – Regatta – Kip

The Greek *spinther* means a spark. The Latin diminutive *scintilla*, a little spark, comes from the same root. From *scintilla* came the verb *scintillare*, to sparkle. For some reason or other this word became *stincillare* among the ordinary people, a verb which gave the Old French *estincelle*, a spark.

The French, notorious for not pronouncing *s*, soon spelled the word *étincelle*. Silk and satin could be made to glitter by weaving gold or silver thread through it: the cloth became *étincelé*. From this was born the English word *tinsel*. Helen Grey from Reading, a fashion designer, wrote to ask.

Stencil also came in a roundabout way from *stincillare*; stencilling, after all, was done to make things sparkle with colour.

An old friend from New Ross has broken a silence that has lasted for 46 years by reminding me of a lovely summer's evening when our world was young. A crowd of us were paddling borrowed *cots* (salmon fishermen's flat-bottomed boats –Irish *coite*) up the Barrow to picnic, and the evening, she says, was for her at least, full of the *étincellement* of romance until yours truly managed to capsize the cot she and I were in, trying to avoid a log.

All is forgiven, it seems, the refreshing swim a fond memory; and what she now wants to know is where the aquatic word *regatta* come from.

It comes from the Venetian dialect word *regatta*. It came into being in a roundabout way. The Latin word *caput*, a head, slid into Late Latin to mean capital (the financial term); and from it came the verb *adcapitare*, to add to capital, to buy.

The French borrowed the word as *achete*, the Italians added *re* and made *recatare* of it, which meant to buy and resell, and later, to haggle. This gave the Venetian word *regatta*, a commercial contention, and this later became an aquatic one.

It seems the word came into English in 1768 when the Earl of Lincoln used it in the invitations he sent his friends to race their boats on his waters.

John O'Brien is a student who lives, he tells me, in a *kip* in Rathmines. He wants to know that the origin of *kip* is.

It was obsolete by 1880 except in Dublin, according to Partridge. It was a brothel, what they used to call in Wexford town a watlin' shop. Compare Danish *kippe*, a brothel, a low tavern.

Hugathepook – Shetland English

In north Mayo many years ago, Cáit Chlinse, who now lives in Eadestown, Naas, Co. Kildare, often herd the word *hugathepook*. She explains it thus: 'North Mayo is a place where the fairies are highly respected, so when one was throwing out dirty water at night, it was the custom to warn the fairies – "Chugaibh, chugaibh an t-uisce salach!" meaning, "To you, to you, the dirty water!" But, on Hallowe'en only, "To you, puca!"'

Cáit tells me people used the Englished version of this last phrase like this: 'He never said hugathepook but turned on his heel and walked off.' In my world, 'Chugat an púca!' (the pooka is coming for you) was said to unruly children.

An interesting creature this púca or pooka or phooka; a cousin of Shakespeare's Puck.

If you want to know more about his history and the great body of folklore surrounding him, get hold of Deasún Breatnach's great book, called, would you believe, *Chugat an Púca*.* He should translate it for a wider audience.

Judge Seán Delap tells me that he recently heard a Donegal man say that he got a good load of *moor* on the shore to put on his potato field. This is Irish, *múr*, a red seaweed found in profusion after a high tide, as Judge Delap knows, being a Gweedore man. What intrigues us both is the word's origin. I wonder could it have come from Norn, the Norse dialect spoken in parts of northern Scotland, Shetland and Orkney until about 1750.

Moor/mur, a dense cover of seaweed, and *múrach*, slab-mud, seaweed, a word from Peadar Ó Conaill's unpublished late 18th-century dictionary, may be related to another *moor/múr* still used in the north and elsewhere: a bank of cloud, a dense shower. Compare

*An Clóchomhar, Baile Atha Cliath, 1993.

the Shetland and Orkney *moorakavie*, a thick fall of drifting snow, where *moor* is related to Icelandic *mor*, fine dust, and the *kavie* element, representing Norwegian dialect *kave*, a heavy snowfall.

Shetland English is a delight. Here's a riddle-rhyme for children, filched from the *New Shetlander*, either written or collected by somebody called Vagaland in 1956:

Da Witch o da Nort, shoo pluckit her geese, An coost the fedders aa awa? — Da witch o da Nort is da caald, caald wind, An da fedders, day're da flukkra snaa.

Flukkra means snow in broad flakes.

Ilk — Stevedore — Handkerchief — Poltroon

Jo MacCarthy of Rochestown, Cork, asks about the origin of the often misunderstood word *ilk*. It is an old word: the 9th-century English as *ilca*, related to *like*, and it survives now only in the title of Scottish landowners, where they took their surnames from their estates. *Guthrie* of that *ilk*, given by Oxford as an example, means 'Guthrie of that same', that is, Guthrie of the place called Guthrie. For somebody to call Jo from Rochestown 'MacCarthy of that ilk' would be nonsense. It is even more nonsensical to say, 'Daniel O'Connell and people of that ilk', as I heard a respected historian say recently in a moment of weakness.

Ena Murphy's husband, a Ringsend man, worked in New York as a stevedor, she tells me. *Stevedore* dates from the 17th century. The word is from Spanish but its remote ancestor was the Latin *stipare*, to pack full, to stow. This gave Spanish *estibar*, to load a cargo, and *estibador*, the man who loads it. Funnily enough some 18th-century dictionaries, not wanting to credit Spain with the newish borrowing, spelled the word *stowadore*.

Handkerchief is bothering Aisling Browne of Sutton. Let's take the last element first. *Chief* is from Latin *caput*; the Greek is *kephale*, and way back we find the Sanskrit *kapala*; it means a head. The *ker* bit is just a little more complicated. The Latin prefix *co-* was used to intensify *operire*, to conceal. This prefix, when it eventually found its way into English, was abbreviated to *cur* (take *curfew*, by way of French *couvre-*

[65]

feu, 'cover fire', as an example). And so it came about that *cur*, spelled *ker*, was added to *chief* to become a medieval woman's head covering. *Handkerchief*, a piece of linen to hold in the hand, came into being in the 16th century.

Poltroon, a wretched coward, a miserable sleeveen, is the subject of a query from Douglas Craig who writes from the Isle of Man. It comes from Middle French *poltron*, from the Italian *poltrone*, a coward, a lie-a-bed, a sluggard, from *poltro*, a bed. *Poltrone* also means colt, because of a colt's habit of bolting. But the word may have emigrated from the barbarians over the Alps in the Dark Ages to give rise to the Italian words. I suggest you compare the Old High German word for a pillow, *bolstar*. It, or the Old Norse *bolstr*, gave English *bolster*, by the way.

Aim's Ace – Hookum-snivey – Gobshite – Slink

Peter Cullen wrote from Laraghbryan, Maynooth, with a few interesting expressions he heard in his youth in rural north Tipperary. The first one is *aim's ace*, and is used of a narrow escape: 'I was within an aim's ace of being killed; I could feel the bull's breath on my neck.'

Aims ace and its other written form *ames ace* should, I suppose, be written *ambs-ace*. This originally meant both aces, or double aces, the lowest possible cast at dice; then it came to mean very bad luck. The French gave us the expression. They said *ambes as*, both aces; and their phrase came from the Latin *ambas*, both, and *as*, smallest unit.

Mr Cullen's other expression is one I've never previously come across: 'A much-used expression was the " the real *hookum snivel* " spoken with regard to something highly suitable. I never came across the expression again until some 60 years later I found it in a P.D. James novel, used by a police sergeant in deepest England.'

In Edgeworth's *Irish Bulls* (1803) we find *Hook-em-snivey*: an indescribable machine, used by boys in playing head and harp. ' "Billy" says I, "Will you sky a copper?" "One", says he. With that I arranged them fair and even with my hook-em-snivey: up they go.'

I can see how the expressions came to be used as one of approval, but I'd like to know what context P.D. James's sergeant used it in. You see, in Devonshire English *hookem-snivey* means deceitful, tricky, sly.

A lady from Naas wrote to ask me if the word *gobshite* is Irish. No, it was imported from England, where it is just as often spelled *gawpshite* and *gaubshite*. They tell me that it is now confined to the county Shakespeare grew up in and to Chester. The EDD glossed the word as a fool, a blockhead; an awkward, ill-kept, dirty person. The second element is from the unattested Old English *scita* of Germanic origin; compare Old Norse *skital*, to defecate, and Middle Dutch *schitte*, excrement. The first element is related to dialect *gaby, gawby, gooby, gorby* etc., a simpleton, a lout, words of unknown origin, I'm sorry to say.

Finally a Letterkenny reader asks about a word she heard from a Scots friend: *slink*, meaning broke, skint. A word of Germanic origin, I'd say. You may compare the Dutch *slinken*, to diminish, to shrink.

Italics

Margaret O'Brien from Ranelagh sent me a copy of a page from *Vanity Fair* of December 1881 which backed a cartoon of Gladstone.

Margaret was tickled by advertisements for Cadbury's Cocoa Essence ('It is often asked, Why does my doctor recommend it? It contains *four times the amount of nitrogenous or flesh-forming constituents* than the average in other cocoas!'): and for the New Remington Type-Writer ('It gives relief from all the physical troubles engendered by the pen, such as pen paralysis, curvature of the spine and lung troubles: the blind, the partially paralysed, and maimed can use it. It opens a new and wide field of congenial labour to educated women').

The New Type-Writer could copy the italic manner of penmanship, so it could: and the ad prompted Margaret to ask what Italy has to do with this.

In 1501 Aldus Manutius of Venice published the works of Virgil, using a type newly-designed by himself, imitating the handwriting of Petrarch. This type became the distinguishing feature of the works published by the Aldine Press. Aldus dedicated his edition of Virgil to Italia – hence the description 'italic'. It differed little either from the modern fount or from the handwriting of the great poet who loved the splendid Laura, a lady who could, methinks, in a later age, have made a blooming fortune advertising Cadbury's Cocoa Essence.

Stigma – Vamp – Snag

The word *stigma*, a moral slur, is one which has its roots in Greek criminal jurisprudence. The Greek word which gave the Latin *stigma* was the verb *stizein*, which meant to mark, the recipient being a criminal who was tattooed with a red-hot iron, both as a punishment and as a means of identification. Runaway slaves were frequent victims.

There was no sense of ignominy in the word's formation, however. Had there been, it would not have been used to denote the marks of Christ's wounds which are said to have appeared on the feet, hands, and sides of people much holier than me, most notably St Francis. Agnes Ryan of Limerick asked about the word.

Bernadette Madden of Shepherd's Bush in London wrote to tell me that the verb *vamp*, in the sense of to vamp an accompaniment on the piano, seems to be in decline.

She recently asked a group of young musicians if they had anybody to vamp for them, and got blank stares in return.

This verb came into English from the Old French *avanpie*, itself from *avant*, before, and *pie*, a foot, from the Latin *pes*.

Avanpie was the front, or foot part of a stocking; it was introduced into English as *vampey*, later shortened to *vamp*.

The verb originally meant to fit with a new vamp, to patch up, in other words. Hence by way of metaphor it came to mean to improvise in a simple, crude way, if céilí band vampers will forgive me.

The other *vamp*, an unscrupulous flirt, an adventuress, is merely a shortening of *vampire*, a word of Slav origin. Serbian has *vampir*.

My contention that the Irish-English *snog*, a slug, is the Irish *snag* (same pronunciation) is right as far as it goes, but it does not go far enough to satisfy a young relative of mine, who points out that the Irish is a borrowing from English.

Snag, a snail, is common from Leicestershire down as far as England's south coast; in east Kent a *snag* is a slug and a snail is a *shell snag*.

Seilmide púca, I suppose, *seilmide* being a snail with a shell. *Ayenbite of Inwyt* (1340) has *snegge*.

From Old High German *sneggo*, all these snags and snogs.

Spoof − *Lampoon* − *Kipe*

Somewhere in George Moore's *Hail and Farewell* he mentions the word *spoof* and speaks approvingly of it, as far as I remember. I was asked recently by Ann McCabe of Clontarf about the word; she and I, and George Moore, would define the word as a mildly-satirical *lampoon* or parody; a good-humoured deception or trick.

But Ann says that increasingly she hears people using the word as if it meant foolish talk, evasive blather, the type politicians use when, not having a clue as to what answer to give to a straight question, start by saying: 'I'm glad you asked me that question.' They then proceed not to answer it in a speech which contains more subordinate clauses than a sentence of the late Cardinal Newman's.

I have noticed this new meaning, too; it has no roots in the word's origin, which is very ordinary indeed. *Spoof* was named for a game involving hoaxing invented and named by one Arthur Roberts, an English comedian, who died in 1913.

Lampoon, by the way, is from French *lampon*, drinking song, from *lampons*, let's drink (a refrain of a drinking song), from the slang *lamper*, to drink. It's in English since the 17th century.

Andrew Lacey wrote from Reading, Berkshire, to ask about a word used on farms and in racing stables by grooms, *kipe*. A *kipe* is a large basket, but the word is used figuratively as well in an indelicate reference to a woman's tummy.

The basket is wider at the top than at the bottom, and Mr Lacey, who hails from south Tipperary, wonders if it is related to the Irish *caidhp*, cap, as it looks like a witch's cap when turned upside down. No. It's from the Old English *cype*. It was a measure for farm produce in the old days in England; it contained about half a bushel. The word is not known in Ireland, as far as I know.

A recent reference to *kip*, a dive, in this column led Roger Ashe, from Bangor, Co. Down, to ask whether I could throw some light on another, unrelated kip, a word used by his father, who hailed from Perth in Scotland. This kip is a verb, meaning to take somebody else's property by violence or by fraud.

The word doesn't seem to have travelled to Ulster. It seems to be Norse in origin. The EDD asks us to compare Norwegian dialect *kippa*, to snatch, snap.

Oul' Mahoun – Kippin' Bag

I am often surprised to find that expressions deemed obsolete in Joseph Wright's great EDD are sent to me by people from the North of Ireland. One such is *Oul' Mahoun*, from Mary Logue who was born near Strabane but is now in exile in Dublin. It was her grandmother's term: she would sprinkle Holy Water copiously on young Mary when she was heading off for dances in Lifford and Letterkenny long ago, to keep Oul' Mahoun at bay, she would say. Your man was the Devil.

Burns, in *The Diel's Away wi' the Exciseman* had 'an ilka wife cry'd 'Auld Mahoun, we wish you luck o' the prize, man.' But Mahoun appeared in Scots literature long before Burns's time. Dunbar, in 1510 or thereabouts, has 'Gramercy', said Mahoun, 'renunce thy God and cum to me.'

Mahoun is a form of Old French *Mahon*, the name of one of the principal devils. *Mahon* is a corruption of *Mahomet*, who wasn't exactly revered in the time of the Crusades. Mary Logue's granny worked in Scotland in the old days; she once shared a field with Paddy the Cope.

Pat McLaughlin, an Inishowen man now living in Haggardstown, Dundalk, was reminded by Andrew Lacey's *kipe*, an agricultural basket, of a word that brings back no fond memories of his own youth.

'When I was a young fellow we used a *kippin' bag*. This was made from a jute sack by the woman of the house. This was used for laying potatoes. The *splits*, sections of potatoes cut for seed, were put into the kippin' bag and you set off laying the splits along the drill, with about two stone weight of splits in the bag. This was one God-awful, back-breaking job for a youngster.'

Macafee's *Concise Ulster Dictionary* had *kibbing bag* and *kippie-bag*. A *kib* was a kind of spade used for planting potatoes in stony or hilly ground where a plough could not work. A pointed pole or staff with a rest for the foot was also used for making the hole into which the splits were dropped.

This instrument was called a *steeveen* in Donegal: the Irish is *stíbhín*, a borrowing from English *stave*, probably. Now it's my guess that *kib*, a borrowing from Scots *kebbie*, a rough walking stick, a shepherd's staff, itself from Old Norse, *keppr*, a cudgel, was once identical with the steeveen: when the potato spade was invented they decided that word *kib* would do rightly for it.

Frippery – Doxy – Heirloom

Frippery is a word I heard recently during a visit to Kilkenny city. A common enough word, you'll tell me, which means cheap, showy clothes, ornaments etc. It can also mean a showing off, a foolish display, pretended refinement.

But the *frippery* I heard spoken of in Kilkenny was a shop which sells old clothes.

'What frippery did she find that dress in, I wonder?' was the remark used by a catty lady in a coffee shop as she eyed a departing acquaintance.

The word brought me back a good many years to the New Ross of my youth, when *frippers* set up their stalls in the Irishtown on fair days to sell clothes to the Secondhand Roses of the town, and there were many of them in those hard times.

I hadn't heard fripper, or the Kilkenny lady's frippery, in half a century. The word comes from Old French *freperie*, from *frepe*, a rag. Further back than that it would be dangerous to venture, although the late Latin *faluppa*, a rag, may well be a cousin.

But the really interesting thing is that the word meant the same to the Kilkenny woman as it did to the Tudor and Jacobean dramatists. A look at the glossaries revealed that Massinger, in *City Madam*, has: 'Here he comes, sweating all over, he shows like a walking frippery'.

And Shakespeare wrote: 'we know what belongs to a frippery' in *The Tempest*.

Anne Byrne, from Arklow, wrote to ask where the word *doxy* comes from. This uncomplimentary word, a favourite of Shakespeare's, was glossed by that old reprobate, John Dunton, in his *Ladies' Dictionary* of 1694: 'Doxies are neither wives, maids, nor widows: they will for good victuals, or for a very small piece of money, prostitute their bodies.' The Wicklow doxy is not a prostitute, Anne tells me, just somebody a little weak in the carnalities, as Seán Ó Faolain put it. The pretty word is a diminutive from *duck*.

The *heir* in heirloom comes, through Old French *heir*, from the Latin *heres*. It is cognate with the Greek *kheros*, bereaved, and reminds us that in law nobody has an heir until he's dead. *Loom*, the word used in weaving, is from Old English *gelomal*, which meant any tool or instrument. Therefore, the first meaning of heirloom is a tool of the family trade handed down from father to son. Margaret Butler, from Carlow, was inquiring.

Louser – Flake

My thanks to Giles Hillson, Whitestrand Road, Galway, to Joan Conroy of Cromwellfort Road, Dublin, and to Brendan Geoghegan of Loughrane Terrace, Mervue, Galway, for solving the problem of *marriages over the tongs*. These marriages, my three correspondents point out, were celebrated in the old days in the blacksmith's forge in Gretna Green. Stepping over the tongs sealed the bargain.

Alf Mac Lochlainn, librarian and scholar, wrote from Galway about the word *louser*. He remembers coming across an anti-Cumann na nGaodhal election flyer which quoted, against him, of course, something Michael Tierney had said about the unemployed: 'The lousers won't work.' Recently he came across a book of Scots verse, published in 1921 in London: *Bonnie Joann and Other Poems*. In it, its author, Violet Jacob, wrote: 'The years are slippin' past ye like water past the bows. Roond half the warld ye've tossed yer dram but sune ye'll have to lowse.' My friend wonders was Tierney, the classical scholar, using the word very correctly, however offensively, to mean 'idlers', and not, as his opponents, thought people infested with lice?

Yes, I have no doubt that louser and lowser are simply variant spellings, and that they have nothing to do with *louse*, the bug (Old English *lús*). The EDD has a couple of pages on *louse / lowse*, a form of 'loose'. It hasn't got *louser*, an idler, but it gives a Yorkshire variant *lowsing*, a noun. To lowse / to loose, means, among other things, to leave off, to stop working, to idle, to lead a vagabond life.

Hence, a pit stopped for the day before the proper or usual time was said to be *lowsed out*. The general idea was to loosen, unfasten, unbind: to lowse cattle was to let them loose to graze: to lowse the table in Yorkshire meant to say grace, so that people could begin to eat. From Middle English *los*, loose, from the Old Norse *lauss*.

John Hall owns a hill farm in Co. Down: he prefers not to say where. He sends me the Down word *flake*, which his father, a Galloway man, also used. It means a temporary gate to close a gap. Vigfusson's dictionary leads me to believe that this is from Old Norse fleki, a hurdle. I am told that in Antrim and in parts of Donegal a *fleki* was an arrangement of branches on which flax was formerly dried over a fire.

Ketchup – Hurley – Drippin' Night

I have rarely seen such an expression of feigned pain on a man's face as I did recently in an excellent Wicklow restaurant when an American visitor asked for ketchup to complement his dinner. The proprietor departed looking grim and returned with the offending goo in a silver sauceboat.

Whatever its merits as a condiment, the word *ketchup*, also found as *catsup* and *catchup*, is Oriental in origin. Collins says that it came from the Chinese (Amoy) *kóetsiap*, the brine of pickled fish, from *kóe*, seafood and *tsiap*, sauce. But let it be said that the late Anthony Burgess thought that this was poppy-cock. He insisted that the word came from Malay *kechap*, to smack with the lips.

Tim Cronin from Douglas, Cork, asks me to settle an argument.

Thus spake Tim: 'I know that as a Wexfordman you are unlikely to know an awful lot about real hurling, but you might be able to tell me which is the correct term for the thing the ball is struck with: is it a hurley or is it a hurl? When I was young we called it a hurl, and hurley was a word you might find used by Camogie players and Cork Con followers. Nowadays it's all hurleys with them, God help us. So now, can you answer my question?'

Both words were in use in the last century; that much I know. Callanan in *The Convict of Clonmel* (1825) has: 'At my bedfoot decaying my *hurl-bat* was lying.' In 1827 Hone called the thing a *hurlet*. This word was from Antrim. Eugene O'Curry in his *Manners and Customs of the Ancient Irish* has: 'He would give his ball a stroke of his hurl ... He would throw his hurl at it.' Eugene was a Clareman: but my friend Jimmy Smyth, the great Clare hurler of the fifties, calls it a hurley. Hall's *Ireland* (1841) calls it a hurley too. I would be interested to know where the thing is called a hurl, and where a hurley today.

Vincent McCann, a Dublinman who lives near me in Wicklow, tells me that in the hard times when he was young Thursday night was known among the working people of the capital as *Drippin' Night*. The maids who worked in the big houses used to save some of the dripping from the roasts and give it to their boyfriends as a thank-you for entertaining them on that night, Thursday being pay-day.

Pettyfogger – Irish Bulls

A barrister friend wrote to ask me what the origin of the word *pettyfogger* is – a word associated with members of his profession. Here we have a contemptuous designation for a lawyer of low class; a person given to underhanded practices. The term appears as early as 1577 in Harrison's *England*, where 'brushes betweene the pettie foggers of the lawes and the common people' is mentioned.

As to *fogger*, its origin is Fugger, the surname of a renowned family of merchant bankers who flourished in Augsburg in the 15th and 16th centuries. The word was absorbed into many European languages.

In 1607, Middleton, in his *Five Gallants*, refers to 'my little German fooker'. Spanish has *fucar*, a contemptuous word for a man of wealth:

German has *fugger, focker* and, saying your presence, *fucker*, in Modern Dutch the term *rijke fokker* is applied to an avaricious man of wealth. The Sussex dialect word *fogger*, meaning huckster, came into being through ironical use, I suppose.

Mrs Jane Reveley of Warnham, Sussex, writes to ask if there is a difference between a *bull* and an *Irish bull*. Her query was prompted by an Elizabeth Barrett Browning quip about Irish bulls.

Well now, a *bull* is an absurd and amusing mistake in language, especially, but not necessarily, one that is self-contradictory, such as 'If you don't get this letter, write and let me know.' The word is of uncertain origin, but you might compare Middle English *bull*, a falsehood, Old French, *boule*, trickery, Icelandic *bull*, nonsense. *Bull* was in use long before Edgeworth's 1802 *Essay on Irish Bulls* associated it with Irishmen; but blunders of the 'Ooops! I wish I hadn't written that' variety should be regarded as bulls, as they would have been pre-Edgeworth (for example Jane Austen's 'Such was Catherine Moreland at ten. At fifteen appearances were mending. She began to cut her hair and long for balls' in *Northanger Abbey*). One of the smarties who laughed at Irish bulls was a lady who wrote this about herself: 'No woman was happier in her choice – no woman. And after above two months of uninterrupted intercourse there is still more and more cause for thankfulness. He loves me better every day, he says. My health improves too.' Who wrote that? Why the newly-married Mrs E.B. Browning herself, would you believe.

Conjuring – Carpenter

The Latin words *jus*, law, and *jurare*, to swear, have a common Sanscrit ancestor in the root *ju*, to join: the link to ancient India hides, therefore, in words such as *justice* and *jury*. This affinity between the words for 'law' and 'oath' is the clue to a major portion of the history of ancient legal ideas. There are, too, interesting overspills, as the Americans say.

Take the word *conjuror*, about which a lady in a Greystones, Co. Wicklow, shopping mall asked me recently.

Conjure comes from *jurare* and *cum*, which means 'with', and so means 'to swear together'. Now, the belief in the ancient world was that if you laid strong spells and swore fierce oaths on the devil, you could call him to help you; indeed, to work wonders for you. The old notion of a conjuror, therefore, was one who conspired with the devil.

John Magowen (or Magowran?) from Monaghan asks why many Irish people stress the second syllable of the word *carpenter*. He asks if the word is French in origin.

To take the last question first, the word is of Celtic origin: compare the Old Irish *carpat* and the modern *carbad*, a chariot. It is thought that when Boadicea first bade the top of the mornin' to the Romans in Britain, the word she would have used for the two-wheeled wagon she was carried round in was *carpentom*.

In Late Latin the contraption was called *carpentum*, and from that they made *carpentarius*, a chariot-builder. Finally, the Normans brought the word back to Britain again as *carpentier*, with the slightly different meaning of any worker in wood. By 1325 it was spelled *carpentere*.

The Irish stress may represent the survival of the old French stress, although it is possible that like the second syllable stress in Anglo-Irish *discipline*, *architecture*, *lamentable* etc., it is due to the influence of the hedge-schoolmasters of the 18th century: men who never had the opportunity to hear standard English spoken, and so had to invent a pronunciation for many strange words they had come across in their reading. Their pronunciations were passed on.

Hedge-school pronunciations have survived modern schooling of all kinds. The late Alan Bliss of UCD defended them, saying the Irish should use their own form of English, which accurately reflects the social history of the country.

Furlong – Plain Sailing – Suff

I am told that once again EU bureaucrats have been pestering the English Jockey Club to get rid of their miles and furlongs; and once again, I am happy to relate, they have been sent packing. The Rowley Mile stays and the Derby distance remains at a mile and four furlongs.

Furlong comes from a very ancient root common to most of the

Aryan tongues. In English the earliest form of the word was *furh*, a furrow; *furlang* in Old English was simply a long furrow.

Commonage in Anglo-Saxon village was divided into long narrow strips, and every freeman would be given an equal number of these, not usually all together. The theory was that ten strips comprised an acre, and every strip was ten times as long as it was broad, making its length, which was the length of the furrow, 220 yards.

I myself remember furrows in West Cork being measured in spades (five and a half feet or two paces; Irish *rámhainn*, a spade). Have they conformed, I wonder?

From the racecourse to the sea. John Byrne of Drimnagh wants to know where the term *plain sailing* comes from. The landlubber's ignorance of the origin of this phrase has given us the spelling plain when it should be plane.

To chart a voyage on a flat sheet must lead to distortion, and the sailor who uses a flat chart for voyages other than short ones must make calculations to allow for the difference between his chart and the curved globe.

A short trip would pose no major problems: this would be plane sailing, sailing using a plane chart, uncorrected. By the way, both plain and plane come from the same Latin word, *planus*, flat.

Another valuable parcel of words has come my way from Jack Foley of Corleagh, Cootehill, Co. Cavan. One is *suff*. An old neighbour of mine used to express contempt for something by saying 'suff on it' or 'suff go deo on it'.

Suff, I'd guess, is a Leitrim pronunciation of the Irish *suth*, given by Dinneen as a variant spelling of *sugha*, soot, both related to Old English and old Norse *sot*, to Old Slavonic *sazda* and to Old Irish *suide*.

Súth has been recorded in the English of Westmeath and *suth* in Roscommon. If you want to insult somebody, Dinneen suggests you try 'a chiaróg shúghaidh – you sooty beetle, your contemptible worm'.

Have a nice day.

Twelfth Night – Gausther – Gowpen

I recently read a book called *The First Night of Twelfth Night* by Professor Leslie Hotson, an American. What ails the man who believes, *contra mundum*, that Twelfth Night is the night following Twelfth Day, and goes on to write a book about it? Let me quote him on page 12: 'The Oxford English Dictionary unhappily defines Twelfth-night as " the evening before Twelfth-day", and is followed in the error by the Fowlers in their Concise Oxford Dictionary, to the misleading of the unwary. One might equally well define "Wedding-night" as "The evening before the wedding day".'

And off the good American professor goes, tripping gaily, unaware of his solecism. Christmas Night, he thinks, is the night following Christmas Day instead of the eve of Christmas Day, our Oíche Nollag too.

I met two old friends of mine in Greystones recently. Ronnie Drew is home for the Christmas and he gave me the word *gawsther*, a word which has a variety of meanings all over Ireland and Britain. As a verb it means to brag, to swagger, to show off: and hence the noun *gausterer*, a boaster, a swaggerer, and the adverb *gausterous*, rude. To *gauster* also means to talk loudly or impudently: hence *gaustering*, laughing out loud.

Gosther to Tyrone's Carleton meant idle talk, gossip: and in Westmeath a *gosther* is a prattler. The word is from Middle English *galstren*, to make a noise. Of Germanic ancestry.

Barney Cavanagh no longer edits the radio news bulletins but he hasn't lost his love of words. He asked me about his northern word *gowpen*, the full of two hands cupped together. There is also the verb, to *gowpen*, to scoop up with both hands. Imported from Scotland this. From the Old Norse *gaupin*, the full of two cupped hands, according to Vigfussen's dictionary

Doctor of Medicine

William Shakespeare used the word *doctor* both of a learned, skilful man and of a physician. Claudio was speaking of the former when he told Don Pedro in *Much Ado*: 'He is then a giant to an ape; but then is an ape a doctor to such a man.'

The whole story of the term *doctor of medicine* is interesting. *Doctor* is the Latin for teacher, and the form in which medieval universities certified the competency of their students was in a licence to teach. In some places the holders of licences were called doctors, in other, masters; the two titles were considered equivalent.

Now it happened that in Salerno, Europe's oldest university, it is said, the only subject taught was medicine, and its graduates were called doctors well before 1000. In the 12th and 13th centuries the Norman ruler of Sicily decreed that the practice of medicine be confined to people holding the teacher's licence of Salerno, and so the licensed teacher and the licensed practitioner became one and the same, and both were called doctor.

Hence came the street use of the word to denote a physician of any grade, whether he or she proceeds to the higher degree of Doctor or not. The barber surgeons, for centuries considered the lowest form of medical life, were allowed the old title of Master, abbreviated to Mr.

I once saw the minutes of a meeting held some time in the early 18th century in Sir Patrick Dun's Hospital (often referred to by the poor of Dublin as St Patrick Dun's) at which the governors gave the masters tally-ho for using the front doors instead of the tradesmen's entrance.

The term 'doctor of skill' is still used of a physician in rural East Anglia, Sussex and Hampshire, to distinguish him from PhDs, DScs and the rest. In parts of Lincolnshire 'doctor' means pharmacist. In Devon and in Cornwall the seventh son of a family without a girl is called 'the doctor'; he is believed to be born with a special aptness for healing. But isn't it strange that to doctor means to mutilate in many places, both here and in England. I heard a man with a pronounced Cork accent shout 'Doctor the bastard!' at the Ireland-Scotland rugby match.

Surgeons are proud to be called Mister, but the dental surgeons now style themselves Doctor to be as good as the medics. Have the barbers nobody to stand up for them?

Dogma – Abominable – Stationers

I read Myles's *The Hair of the Dogma* again recently, and great fun it is. Now *dogma* is an interesting word, not connected at all with *doctrine* which comes from the Latin *docere* to teach. The Greeks gave us *dogma*, which comes from *dokein*, to seem good. Its nearest relative is the Latin *decet*, it is seemly, from which we got the English *decent*. Dogma once upon a time meant 'that which seems good to one', an opinion held. But when the great Councils of the Church met to discuss matter of great importance, they sought a consensus of opinions. The opinions held in common by the orthodox bishops were called dogmas, but soon the word took the meaning of a belief taught or held as the authoritative truth.

Lexicographers sometimes lose the run of themselves, and when they issue dogmas in relation to etymologies that prove to be false strange things happen to words. Take the word *abominable*. Medieval scholars thought the word came from the Latin *ab homine*, 'from a man' spelled it *abhominable*, and glossed it as 'repulsive to mankind'.

That's how the word got its modern meaning. The trouble is that the word really came from the Latin *omen* coupled with the *ab*, away from, which gave the Latin adjective *abominabilis*, ill-omened. The Old French borrowed the word as *abominable*, but not long after it came into English the grammarians came to the wrong conclusion as to its origin and inserted the intrusive *h*.

Mary O'Connell from Douglas, Cork, recently noted that the city shop in which she buys the *Irish Times* has changed from being a Stationer to a Newsagent. She wonders if *stationer* is soon to become a redundant word, and asks about the word's origins.

'To stand' in Latin was *stare*, and that gave the noun *statio*, a standing-place, in Late Latin we find *stationarius*, a soldier having a fixed post, generally a post-master at a military post-station. Subsequently a *stationarius* came to mean a tradesman who kept a shop in one place, and who didn't move about from market to market, from fair to fair, to peddle his wares, as was the norm in those days.

In the course of time the great universities licensed permanent booksellers in the medieval towns they controlled. These booksellers traded from permanent shops, and in Oxford and Cambridge became Stationers to the Universities — the forerunners of the stationers we know today.

Crevin — Free — Stell

Geraldine Murtagh from Tobercurry, Co. Sligo, has written to say that she hopes that I can shed some light on two words that she remembers from her childhood and teens in north Leitrim. The first of these is *crevin*, used to describe the mound of turf which extends above the top edge of the trailer.

Crevin is from the Irish *craoibhín* which means, according to Dinneen, 'a row of turf sods put standing upright around and above the mouth of a creel to keep in the smaller peat'. Dinneen found the word in the Rosses and Gweedore, Co. Donegal; Geraldine has found it in Sligo as well as in her native Leitrim.

Her second word is *free*. I'll let the lady speak for herself: '*Free* is the neat, block-like wall of turf holding the fuel in a shed or stack. The older generation took great pride in *freeing* the stack of turf so that it would stand firm against the winter gales.'

This *free* of Geraldine's also comes from Irish. *Fraigh*, Dinneen tells us, is a Connacht word, meaning among other things, 'the clamp or retaining course of a turf rick'. Two more Irish words from the English of Ireland, until now unknown to me. Delighted to have them.

Patrick Hunter Blair of Mountcaper, Spa, Ballinahinch, Co. Down, tells me that there is another *stell* (from the same source as *stillion* probably) in everyday use among Galloway sheep farmers, and, I should think, among some of their kin in the north of Ireland.

Patrick writes: 'A stell is a shelter of dry-stone walls (called *dykes*), built on an open hill. The stells may be rectangular, circular, T-shaped or cruciform. They may be any size from 5 to 30 yards across. Many of them are reputed to have been built by prisoners of war in Napoleonic times, when sheep farming as it is practised today started to develop in that part of Scotland.' The EDD has: *stell-dykes*, the wall of an enclosure for sheep.

Patrick goes on: 'Stells should not be confused with *buchts*, sheep-handling pens made from dykes. Buchts tend to be close to the *steading* (farmyard) and can be a complex collection of small enclosures, corridors and gates. I hope that these thoughts from a hill farmer's son are of interest to you.'

Bucht I've heard in Donegal. It's from Flemish *bocht*, a sheep-fold. Thanks, Patrick.

God's Own Country – Teetotaller – Pamphlet

Brendan Ryan from Old Lucan Road, Palmerstown, Dublin asks me where the phrase *God's own country* originated, knowing that inebriated citizens of many countries including our own have in times of national celebration put their own tag on the silly phrase.

Oxford tells me that the phrase, in a slightly shortened version, *God's country*, was first used nostalgically of home by northern troops fighting in the mosquito-infested marshes of the deep south during the American Civil War. Not until the 1880s did the phrase come to mean the prairies. I once received a brochure inviting me to holiday in a place near Skibbereen, described with the diffidence the natives have been noted for since Tsarist times as 'the Acapulco of the South, set in God's own country'.

Monica Cleere from Kilkenny wants to know what the tee in *teetotaller* comes from. The Latin word *totum* means 'the whole'. In an old gambling game in which a kind of gig or top was used, one of several faces of the top was marked T for totum, signifying that the player who had spun the top to land with the T facing upwards could scoop the pot.

The top itself was called *teetotum*, and no doubt the existence of this slang word suggested teetotal as an emphatic form of total. Teetotal, it seems, was first used in the United States in the early 19th century but it gained currency in Britain and in Ireland due to the speeches of Mr Dicky Turner of Preston, who could claim to be the Father Mathew of Lancashire. Dicky died, sober, in 1833, and the inscription on his tombstone claims that he was the first to have used the word teetotal, as applied to a person who doesn't drink, in one of the pamphlets he was fond of writing for the benefit of the Irish navvies who didn't appreciate him one little bit.

Pamphlet – an interesting word this. *Pas*, plural *pantes*, is the Greek for 'all', *philein* means 'to love'. In the 12th century a spicy Latin love poem called *Pamphilus*, meaning 'loved by all', was an international hit.

A manuscript copy of the poem was a good deal less bulky than that of an ordinary book, and in time it became known familiarly as a pamphlet – the *et* being the now familiar diminutive ending. Pamphlet was soon used to describe any little book of similar size.

Fritter – The Dog's Letter – Snog

Hazel Hall from Priestfield Road, Edinburgh, was making fritters the other day when the thought came to her to ask me whether there could be a connection between the word for apples dipped in batter and fried in deep fat, the *fritter* that mean small pieces, and the verb that means to break into small pieces.

Fritter, the food, is from Old French *friture*, from Latin *frictus*, fried, from *frigere*, to fry. The other *fritter* is, according to Collins, an 18th-century word, probably from obsolete *fitter*, to break into little pieces, ultimately from Old English, *fitt*, a piece, eighteenth century? Does nobody at Collins read Shakespeare any more? Do they not remember Falstaff having a laugh at the Welshman Evan's pronunciation of cheese and butter in *The Merry Wives of Windsor*: 'Seese and putter! Have I liv'd to stand at the taunt of one that makes fritters of English?'

Hazel had a second question. She is a fan of Leonardo di Caprio and urges me to buy the video of *Romeo and Juliet*. She once took part in a school production of the play, she tells me, but it is so long ago that she has forgotten what the following exchange means:

Nurse: Doth not rosemary and Romeo begin both with a letter?
Romeo: Ay, nurse, what of that?; both with an R.
Nurse: Ah, mocker! That's the dog's name.

[83]

R, the dog's letter, from its resemblance in sound to the snarling of a dog, was a familiar idea in Shakespeare's time. Jonson, in his *English Grammar*, says: 'R is the dog's letter and hurreth in the sound.'

In *Ship of Fools* (1578) we find, 'This man malicious which troubled is with wrath. Nought els soundeth but the hoorse letter R. Though all be well, yet he none answer hath Save the dogges letter glowing with nar, nar.'

There you are, Hazel. I sincerely hope that Leonardo didn't follow the current trend of pronouncing Juliet's name as if she had been a French girl.

Among the interesting words sent to me by a regular correspondent from Cavan, James Maguire, is the word *snog*. A snog, he says, is 'a low-down cur of the human variety'. James has never heard the word outside Cavan and Monaghan.

This is the Irish word *snag* (pronounced 'snog'), defined by the incomparable Dinneen as 'a snail, a creeping thing or person, a crawler'.

Swashbuckler – Antics

J. O'Flaherty of Galway wrote about the expression used in Munster Irish, *ag ól tobac* – drinking tobacco. Could it possibly be a borrowing? he asks.

Yes, the Jacobeans drank their tobacco. Hawkins the sailor, writing in 1622 in *Voyage to the South Sea*, explains: 'With drinking of tobacco it is said that the Reobucke was burned in the range of Dartmouth.' The verb drink is from Old English *drincan* and has cognates in Old Norse *drekka* and Old Saxon *drinkan*. Hawkins and his contemporaries considered smoking as a pouring of tobacco down the throat, and hence their use of the verb to drink.

Hawkins was a swashbuckler of note, a word with a great sound to it. Margaret O'Brien of Corbally, Limerick, would like to know whether a swashbuckler is a man who swashes buckles or one who buckles swashes.

Bucca was the Latin for a cheek, especially a cheek puffed out with food or with breath (the French borrowed the word as *bouche*, a mouth). Bucca had a diminutive, *buccula*, which in Late Latin came to mean a rounded projection or boss. This buccula gave us *buckle*, and also *buckler*, a round shield protected with a boss. *Swash* is imitative of the sound swords made when swishing through the air: and swashbuckler, therefore, is a chap who, like his Irish counterpart *buaileam sciath*, swashes at his enemy's shield, with the implication that he does little damage but makes an awful lot of noise. Swashbuckler dates from the sixteenth century. In 1560 a long-forgotten writer called Pilkington wrote: 'To be a dronkarde, a gambler, a swashe-buckeler, he hath not alowed thee one mite.'

J. Power of Ferrybank, Waterford, is a man who enjoys the *antics* of the Spice Girls.

Back we go to the Latin *antiquus*, ancient, from which English borrowed *antique*. But the same word went into Italian as *antico*, which was the name given to one of the ancient subterranean Roman workings. From there it was transferred to the grotesque carvings on its walls, and so came to mean simply 'grotesque'. This is the meaning it has in Italian Renaissance literature, and so it was borrowed as *antic* by the Elizabethans. Hamlet's 'antic disposition' shows a stage in the transition to the sense 'grotesque behaviour'. From there it is just a hop to the Spice Girls' considerably more sexy antics.

Gobaloon − Immis − Protagonist

'What exactly is a *gobaloon*?' asks Mary O'Connor of Waterford city. 'The reason I ask is that here a gobaloon is a class of gom, a harmless fellow for all that, and you should note that there are no female gobaloons among us. To friends of ours from near Loughrea, Co. Galway, the word means a dunderhead. But back in west Waterford a gobaloon is something else entirely: a thieving class of a sleeveen. Is gobaloon a corruption of some Irish word, itself from the Norman French?'

I don't think it is, although the *-oon* ending seems to indicate a Norman connection. (Consider *bosthoon*, Irish *bastún*, originally Norman French *baston*, a stick, etc.), I think the word's origin is French all right, but modern: *gobe-a-l'eau*, one who seizes (anything)

[85]

on the water. This has come into the dialects of southern England as *gobbalew*, a coastguard in Hampshire, an exciseman in Devon and Cornwall: and because people who followed those occupations weren't exactly popular in the old days, the term gained currency as a generic one for anybody thoroughly disapproved of.

Jane Crane of Dunlewy, Co. Donegal, sends me a word she heard used by a man who spent many years working in Scotland. This old man remarked: 'Isn't it an immis kind of a day' when he meant that the day was changeable. *Immis* is sometimes found as *emmis* or *eemis*. Of land, or of seed, the word means variable in its productive results. It can also mean rickety, so that you may still hear in Burns's country, 'That auld ladder is eemis.' From the Old Norse *ymiss*, various, alternate, it survives in Swedish as *ymsa*, to change.

Dermot O'Neill writes from Rathfarnham about the often misused *protagonist*. The Greek for 'to bring' was *agein*, and so *agon* meant a bringing together of people, particularly for a meeting such as the Olympic games. From this they derived *agonistes*, a competitor. The fiercely competitive world of Greek drama borrowed the word and an actor also came to be known as *agonistes*. In the early dramas there was only one actor and a chorus: when a second was added, the words *protos* and *deuteros*, first and second, were combined to make *protagonistes* and *deuteragonistes*. A protagonist is therefore the principal character and there cannot be two of them. And he is not, as is often thought, a champion or an advocate.

Mollag – Dwees – Pillock

Mr Leslie Doyle, who lives in Claydane, Manchester, but who was born and bred in Greystones, sent me two interesting words. The first is *mollag*, found only in the Isle of Man, it seems. Mollag is a dog's skin blown up as a bladder and used as a buoy to float herring nets in the old days. And when a Manxman tells you that he's full as a mollag, he means that he is what Mayo and Kent people might describe as *disguised*, that is, drunk. Mollag is a native Manx word.

Mr Doyle's second word, he heard in his native Greystones. I'm sure he won't mind me mentioning that he is boarding on the four score, as they say in Galway and in Warwickshire; and in the course of his letter he recalls discussing the word *dwees* with an old Wicklow fisherman not long ago. Let me quote him: 'Greystones had a considerable fishing industry in the 19th century and to a much lesser extent up to the 1930s. Fishermen there used a dog's skin, blown up and tarred, as a bladder. This they used as a float, and one was placed at each end of a trammel net or long line, to mark, on the surface, the ends of the net and line. I have never known the origin of the word which, I think, was not confined to Greystones fishermen. That fact that the finished bladder was black and that the Irish for black is *dubh* may be a pointer.'

I don't think so. Perhaps we should look to the English dialect word *dwyes*, always found in the plural. In the Isle of Wight, *dwyes* are eddies, but in Cornwall the older fishermen have transferred the word to the glass floats that bob on them. Dwyes and dwees. I wonder am I putting two and two together and making five? Dwees are *blandies* in Kerry. Used of corpulent men and women as well as floats. Where that came from I don't know. Irish speakers have *bleaindí*.

An Anglican clergyman whose name I would not divulge for all the taa (that is, Wexford tea) in China, asks where his wife's words for a man she doesn't like, *pill* and *pillock*, come from. Modern slang? Well, they survive in modern slang, certainly. But they are old Scandinavian imports, considered naughty words once. From Norse *pill*, membrum virile, I'm afraid.

Harbinger — Crowner — Osteopath

George Mitchell, God help him, was recently referred to in one of the papers as a 'harbinger of peace'. He's hardly that: a harbinger is a person or thing that goes ahead to announce the approach of someone or something: a forerunner. No matter, harbinger is an old word and its origin is pointed to in the Middle English *herbengar* and the Old French *herbergere*, provider of shelter. Its roots are Teutonic, *heri*, an army, and *berga*, protection. The word *harbour* is made from the same elements, and indeed harbour originally meant a place *on land* where an army might take refuge. Herbengar or harbinger was the man sent on ahead to find a harbour for the army, a billeting officer. Nowadays the use of the word is exclusively metaphorical.

Andy Regan of Bishopstown, Cork, was intrigued at finding the word *crowner* used by Shakespeare and glossed as 'coroner' in the footnotes to whatever edition he possesses. What, he asks, has either word to do with sudden death?

Both words meant simply a representative of the crown, from Latin *corona* through Anglo-French *corouner*. Richard I appointed the first coroners as keepers of the pleas of the crown: in other words, their job was to see that the crown got its financial rights and that prime boys hadn't boodle that belonged to Dick deposited on the quiet.

Richard wasn't a man for the shilly-shallying of judicial tribunals and the like; if you were caught fiddling it meant that somebody was told to sharpen the axe. A corpse, therefore, was of interest to the king's revenue commissioners, because if a successful prosecution followed treason (messing with the king's revenue was regarded as such), or murder, the miscreant's possessions went to the exchequer. The crown also had claims on treasure-trove: this is why you'll still see the queen's coroners involved with cases of this nature as well.

King Richard could have ostracised the tax-dodgers of course instead of using the more direct method. In ancient Athens when two politicians clashed in such a manner as to threaten the peace, a ballot was taken, and the loser left the place for a time, usually ten years.

The votes were written on potsherds (*ostraca*) which has the same root as *ostreon*, a bone, from which we get words such as *osteology* and *osteopath*. So the process of saying bye-bye to Athens was called *ostracismos*, just a small step from the English word.

Back-friend – Buck

For some time back I have been collecting words that have survived in the English of Ireland since Tudor times. Last week two more arrived in the post to me.

The first is from J.S. Poyntz from Sutton and it's a word he heard many times in Sligo when he was much younger than he is now. His word is *back-friend*, and it means a secret enemy, a back-stabber, a sleeveen intent on malice. John Florio has the word in the great dictionary he dedicated to Anne of Denmark, James the First's wife: 'Inimico, an enimie, a foe, an adversarie, a back-friend'.

Surprise, surprise, Shakespeare has the word as well in *The Comedy of Errors*: Dromio of Syracuse, in answer to a civil question, says that his master is 'in Tartar limbo, worse than hell. A devil in an everlasting garment hath him; one whose hard heart is buttoned up with steel; a fiend, a fairy, pitiless and rough; A wolf, nay worse, a fellow all in buff; A back-friend, a shoulder-clapper.'

The second word comes from J. Connolly of Artane who heard the word *buck* used by old men who worked in the Poulmounty woollen mills, between Borris and New Ross, many years ago.

Buck, considered by the EDD to be obsolete or close to it almost a hundred years ago, is still very much alive in places in the south-east of Ireland. It was a word for lye, made from stale urine or wood ashes, or cow-dung, for washing wool or coarse linen. It also meant a large wash of clothes. Hence the old people had the words *buckbasket*, a washerwoman's clothes basket; *bucklee*, the lye of wood ashes, a commodity never brought into the house during the Christmas; *buck-house*, a washing house, a laundry (a northern Irish word this, recorded from an advertisement in the Belfast *Newsletter* of 1738).

Now as to the Tudors, Shakespeare has 'Buck! I wish I could wash myself of the buck' in *The Merry Wives of Windsor*, and relating to a wash of clothes, has 'she washes bucks here at home' in *Henry VI, Part 2*. *Buck* is far older than Tudor times. *Piers Plowman* has '[He] laueth hem in the lauandrie and bouketh hem at his brest.' Its origin? The Middle English *bouken*, from Low German *buken*. Interestingly, the Irish is *buac*, lye.

The Dickens — Dawn — Paradise

Ms Mary O'Neill, from the town of Dungannon, wonders where the dickens the phrase *What the Dickens?* comes from. Is it older than Charles, the novelist, she wonders?

The *dickens*, in what was once a petty oath, is probably a corruption of *devilkins*. Mrs Page, answering Ford in *The Merry Wives of Windsor*, says: 'I cannot tell what the dickens his name is my husband had him of.' Further back than this I can't go, I'm afraid.

That lovely word *dawn* is of interest to a young lady, Ms Jacqueline Hunt, who is writing a transition-year paper in physics. All she wants from me is information as to the word's origin, thank God – as a physicist I never quite made the grade, any grade.

The word is short for *dawning*, from Old English *dagian*, to dawn. The *daw* part is interesting: to daw meant to become day. Both daw and day are derived from the same root as the Sanskrit *dah*, to burn. The Aryans long ago saw the dawn as the flame burning in the east, and so it became personified as *Dahana*, the flaming one. The Greeks borrowed Dahana as *Daphne*, which means laurel, the virgin daughter of the river-god, Peneios.

She was chased by the sun-god, Apollo, who was desperately in love with her. Ovid told her story memorably in *Metamorphoses*: her father, answering her prayer, changed her into a laurel tree, and poor old Apollo, when he finally caught up with her, could feel her heart fluttering beneath the bark. Henceforth, the god declared, the laurel, *Daphne*, would be associated with glory.

The myth has inspired many great works of art, Jacqueline, notably Bernini's superb baroque sculpture which shows Daphne being pursued by Apollo, and the Renaissance painter Pollaiuolo's depiction of Daphne being transformed into a laurel tree as poor Apollo arrives too late.

Start chasing a word and God only knows where you'll end up. Take Ms Audrey Dalton's *paradise*. In old Persian, *diz* means to mould and *pairi* is equivalent to the Greek *peri*, which begins many English words, such as *perimeter*, and means 'around'.

Paradaeza means a place fenced around: the pleasure gardens of a Persian nobleman, in particular. Xenophon introduced the word into Greek as *paradeisos*, and the translators of the Bible into Greek, finding no word for a place of perfect bliss, and knowing no people as given to luxury as the Persians, chose Xenophon's word to represent heaven.

Mystery – Chaperone – Hazard a Guess

The word *mystery* has an interesting history, I am glad to tell a transition-year student in a Dublin school who asks about it.

To pronounce the Greek letter *mu* – our M – you must compress your lips as if you were about to pout, or make a *moue*, as the French have it. That *mu* gave rise to the verb *muo*, which means 'I put my lips together'.

In ancient Greece some ceremonies of a religious nature were held in front of people who were sworn to secrecy: such a person was called *mustes* because he had to keep his lips shut tight on the secret. The religious rituals themselves were called either *musteria* or *mysteria* in relation to the Sacraments, and so *mystery* took on the sense of 'that which has a hidden significance'.

No names, dear reader, as you requested. Mum's the word! Now you know the history of that *mum*, too, a word suggestive of closed lips, and in English since the 14th century by way of the above.

The word *chaperone* is, I was not very surprised to hear, almost obsolete; Jane Kelly of Youghal asks about its pedigree.

Its history starts with the ecclesiastical vestment called in English the cope. In late Latin it was *cappa*, which comes from the root of *caput*, a head. The French borrowed this word as *chape*, and this had a diminutive, *chaperon*, a kind of hood which became very fashionable in Renaissance times. The original Little Red Riding Hood was *Le Petit Chaperon Rouge*.

The modern sense of chaperone comes from the notion of an older lady protecting a younger one, as a hood protects the head or face. The word should be spelled *chaperon*, of course. Because the word was used metaphorically of a woman, the English decided to give it a feminine ending in *e*.

John O'Riordan of Cork's Blackrock wants to know where the expression *to hazard a guess* originated. There is no doubt that a gambling game called in Latin *azardum*, in Italian *azzardo*, in Old French *hasard*, and in English *hazard* arose in the time of the Second and Third Crusades. The origin of the word is the Arabic *az-zahar*, to die.

Hooking It

A man from Belleen, Nenagh, Oiliféar Ó Muirí by name, is puzzled by the expression he heard in south Roscommon where he grew up: 'He wasn't long hooking it out of there' – said of somebody who left in a hurry.

'To hook it' is as common in England and in Scotland as it is here. Dickens has 'He gave me four half bulls and ses Hook it!' in *Bleak House*, while, up north, Scott and a host of others considered it dialect, not slang. It was an English or Scottish spailpín's expression: when a man said that he would take his hook or sling his hook or that he was going to hook it, he meant that he was about to head off to a hiring fair with a scythe or a reaping hook.

Later these expressions came into slang and cant use. The EDD gives 'When he saw the policeman he slung his hook', meaning he took off: Carew, in his *Autobiography of a Gipsy* (1897) has 'When I was about fourteen I slung my 'ook and joined some travellin' Barks': by the middle of the century 'to hook it', meaning simply to leave in a hurry, was common all over Britain, Ireland and America, and used by people who wouldn't know a reaping hook from a flail.

Thanks to Jimmy McGill of Claremont Road, Howth, to Pat Walsh of Ballybofey, to Kevin Bright of Goodwin's Hill, Batterstown, Co. Meath, and to Dr Seán Ua Conchubhair from Uarán Mór, Galway, for pointing out to me that my guess as to the origin of *jildy* (Kipling has it as *juldee*) was about 3,000 miles off the mark.

It comes not from Old Norse but from Hindi and was brought here by Irishmen who fought in British regiments in India. But there is this to add: my *gildr* and *jildy* come from the same ancient Indic root.

Many interesting words arrived here during Christmas. Jack Foley of Corbeigh, Cootehill, Co. Cavan, tells me that a *reefer* in his part of the country is not what you might think. No, this was the name of a 'four-swing' in a céilí dance or a set. A valued correspondent from Glenariffe tells me that a *trinket* is a small water channel, much smaller than a *sheugh*. Of French origin this.

Compare the Normandy dialect word *trenque*, itself from Central French *trenche*, now obsolete, from which *trench* came.

Frack – Greeking – Flake – Words from Jack Devereux

An honest Ulsterman by the name of John McArthur has sent me a brace of interesting words from the Sperrins, where his mother came from. The first of them is *frack*. It means a blister.

The *Concise Ulster Dictionary* doesn't have this word but there is a Scots word *farack*, a small mark on the skin, a word that comes from Old Norse *far*, a mark, track or print. I have little doubt that *frack* is related to another dialect word, *freck*, a verb that means to mark with spots, to dapple. My old friend John Clare has this in a poem of 1821: 'In whose margins flags were freckt'; and again in the same poem, 'The eve put on her sweetest shroud, Frekc'd with white and purple cloud.'

Another word that undoubtedly came to Ulster from either the north of England or Scotland is *greeking*: the *greeking* of the day is the dawn. Scott has a note on this greeking, sometimes spelled *greiking*, but Douglas had it back in 1513 in *Eneados*: 'Quhen the quene The first greking of the day has sene.' This is a derivative of Old Norse *gryja*, to dawn. Compare Danish and Swedish *gry*.

Jack Reid comes from the Isle of Man to Greystones every Christmas and he gave me the word *flake*, a sandy patch among submerged rocks. I had heard of this word; Manx folklore has it that mermaids sleep in the flakes and that they lure good-looking sailors down there for a bit of how's-your-granny-for-slack. Again, this is a Norse word; compare Norwegian dialect *flak* and *flag*.

My old friend, the fisherman Jack Devereux of Kilmore Quay, died just before Christmas. He gave me over the course of time many good words that had been overlooked by the lexicographers. *Soustrum*, he told me, is the south-going tide; *norstrum* is the tide that flows north. Compare the Dutch *stroom*, the German *strom*; *Traams*, the end-pieces in the shafts of a cart; Middle Dutch and Middle Low German *trame*. *Waur*, to notice. 'I didn't waur you going by.' This from Old English *warian*. He never said 'this morning'; it was always 'today mornin'. *Wingeens*, plural, was his word for flotsam. I have no idea as to its origin, nor do I know where his *pulmare* came from, 'an untilled pathway between crops in a field, between barley and oats, for example.' I'll miss him, God look to him.